The One BIBLE

365 stories & prayers

Stories retold by L. M. Alex

Prayers by Anne K. Clark

Illustrations by Gustavo Mazali

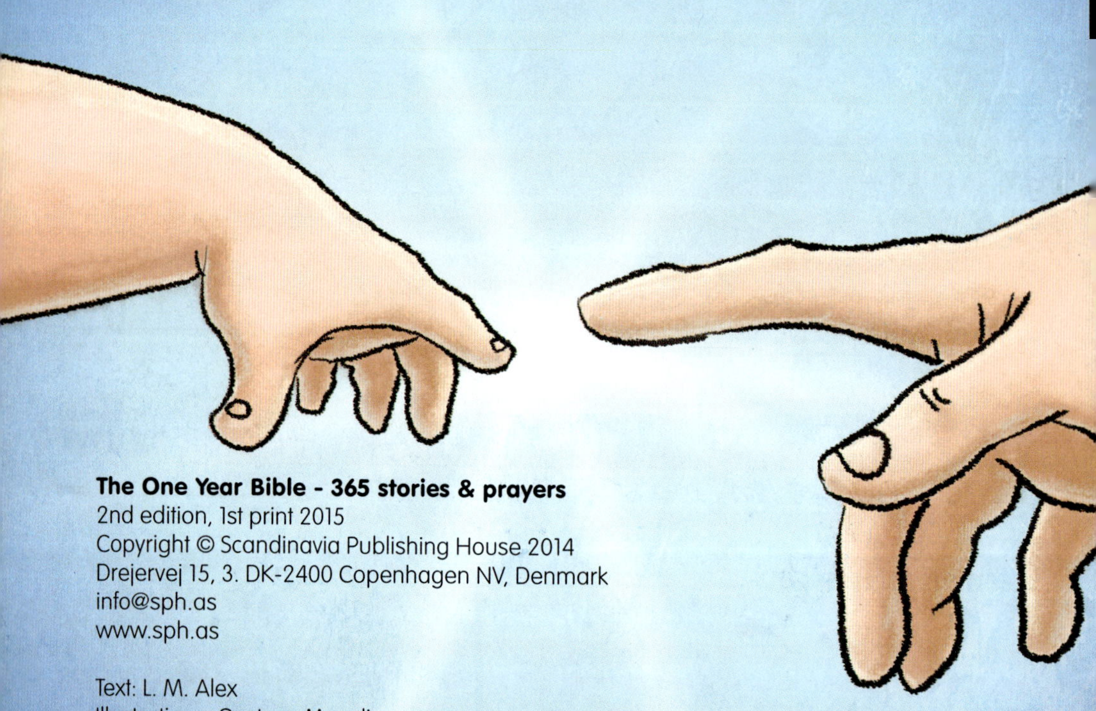

The One Year Bible - 365 stories & prayers
2nd edition, 1st print 2015

Drejervej 15, 3. DK-2400 Copenhagen NV, Denmark
info@sph.as
www.sph.as

Text: L. M. Alex
Illustrations: Gustavo Mazali
Prayers: Anne K. Clark
Editor: Cecilie Fodor
Graphic Design: Isabelle Gao & Hanyu Gao

Printed in China
ISBN: 9788771321425

The One Year BIBLE

365 stories & prayers

Stories retold by L. M. Alex
Prayers by Anne K. Clark
Illustrations by Gustavo Mazali

Contents

DAY 1

The First Day

Genesis 1:1-5

It was all about to begin. There was not yet an earth. There was not yet a sun or a moon. In every place . . . in every space . . . all was as dark as can be. But even in darkness, God was there. And God had a plan. "Let there be light!" said God. And there was light. Across all of space, it shined the rays of God's good love.

Dear God, Help me not to be afraid of the dark because You are with me, and You made the light. Amen.

Heaven and Earth

Genesis 1:6-8

It was day number two. God made the heavens, and God made the earth. In between them was the wide, open sky. Now there was night, and there was day. Now there was heaven, and there was earth. And just like always . . . there was God.

Dear God, You were here before there was anything. You are the most powerful one. Thank You for loving me. Amen.

The Sea and Sky

Genesis 1:9-13

God was making the world. On day three, God made the seas. He called for land to rise up from the water. "Let there be grass," said God. "Let there be plants and trees." Each had seeds for making more. So the earth began to grow with living things. God looked at what He had made and saw it was good.

Dear God, You made everything good. Thank You for
making the clouds and sky and water and trees. Amen.

The Sun and Moon

Genesis 1:14-19

It was day four. God filled the sky with stars to give light to the earth during nighttime. The biggest light of all would shine for day. This was the sun. Another would shine at night. This light was the moon. God looked out over all He had made. And God knew that it was good.

Dear God, You made the light for the day and lights for the night. It helps me to remember that You are always here with me. Amen.

Birds and Fishes

Genesis 1:20-23

The world was about to come alive. God said, "Let the sea fill with fish. Let the sky fill with birds." God made mighty whales. He made every animal of the water. God made birds that would run and hop and fly. God smiled on all He had made. God saw that it was good. "May you be more and more," He told the fish and the birds. And so it was.

Dear God, All the birds and fish You have made are so amazing. I love all the different ones. Amen.

DAY 6

God Makes the Animals

Genesis 1:24-26

Next, God made animals. Some to walk and some to slither. Some to creep and some to swing from high above. Last of all, God made people. He made man and woman so they were like him. Of all the fish of the sea and the birds of the sky, the animals that walked and the animals that crept, it was people who were going to be the ones in charge.

Dear God, Thank You for creating all the animals on
the earth. They are so unique and wonderful. Amen.

Life Begins

Genesis 2:1-7

It was day number seven. God was done making the world. He had filled it full of wonders . . . with the sea, the sun, plants, and animals. Now, it was time to rest. God blessed the seventh day. In the garden the animals were running around, and the grass and plants were growing. The trees were stretching their branches to the sky, and the rivers were bubbling with life. A man and a woman also came to life. It was Adam and Eve. They opened their eyes for the very first time. And they saw what a wonderful world God had made.

Dear God, All that You have made in nature makes me so happy. Thank You for making it so beautiful. Amen.

DAY 8

The Garden

Genesis 2:8-3:24

Adam and Eve lived in the Garden of Eden. It was a wonderful place full of animals and plants and good things to eat. There was just one rule. God said, "No eating from the tree in the middle of the garden." One day, Adam and Eve got curious. Why was this tree so special? They tasted the fruit . . . not bad at all! Yet God can see all things, and God was so sad. He told them they had to leave the perfect garden. From now on, Adam and Eve would work for their food. Even still, God would watch over them. Even still, God would love them very much.

Dear God, Your love never stops. When I make a bad choice, thank You that You still love me. Amen.

The Very First Children

Genesis 4:1-7

God is never done with giving surprises. Soon enough, Eve had a belly that was big and round. Little Baby Cain was born as a gift from God. Then came a brother named Abel. Adam and Eve were full of joy for their two small sons. God sure was good. The two boys grew and grew. Like all children, each one was special. Each one had something they were good at. Cain became the farmer while Abel watched the sheep.

Dear God, Thank You for giving us wonderful surprises. Everything good comes from You. Amen.

DAY 10

Two Brothers

Genesis 4:8-17

Abel walked around with a big, happy smile. Cain was starting to worry. Did God love his brother more than him? Cain got more and more jealous. Until one day, Cain killed his brother. Then he tried to hide the truth. God knows every secret, of course. And He knew just what it was that Cain had done. God sent him away to wander in the desert alone. How very sorry he was. Cain prayed, and God was listening. God said he would keep Cain safe, and one day, Cain would have a family of his own.

Dear God, Grace means being loved even when I do bad things. Thank You God for Your grace and for loving me all the time. Amen.

A Big, Wide World

Genesis 6:1-10

Families began to grow. People moved to new lands. God started the world by first making light, and now it was a place shining with color. But people were starting to forget about God. They no longer listened to hear God's voice. They stopped believing and did evil, wicked things. This made God very, very sad. A man named Noah looked at all the beautiful things that God had made, and Noah smiled because God was good. Noah was different because he believed in God and didn't do evil and wicked things like the people around him.

Dear God, Help me to remember You and to listen for You. Thank You for always remembering me. Amen.

DAY 12

Noah Builds a Boat

Genesis 6:11-22

Noah loved God with all his heart. So when God told him to build a boat, Noah obeyed. Noah built a big and sturdy boat. God told him to fill the boat with animals, two by two. Noah's family found two of each animal and put them on the boat. "Silly, Noah!" people said. Then they went their way, not caring one bit about God or what He had to say. This made God very sad, and it was the reason He was starting the world over again.

Dear God, Sometimes Your plan might seem funny and strange. Help me to know that You are the leader in charge. Amen.

The Boat without a Sea

Genesis 7:1-16

Every animal was on board the boat. Then Noah's family went in, and God shut the door. It looked very strange to see such a big boat on dry land. There was not even a pond nearby . . . let alone an ocean! Then it began to rain; water was falling from the sky! Just a little at first and then the drops got bigger and bigger. Soon, water rose around the boat. Maybe Noah had been right all along.

Dear God, I don't always know the answers, but You know everything. I will do what you tell me to do. Amen.

A Sea without End

Genesis 7:17-8:8

It rained, and it rained, and it rained. For forty days and nights, the earth filled with water. The rivers and lakes got wider and wider until there was no ground left. Then even the mountains were covered by the sea. At last, all was still. Noah peeked out. The rain had stopped. Yet now they floated on a wide, open sea. Was there any place for the boat to land? Noah would send a bird to go find out. He took one of the doves and set it free to see if it could find anywhere dry to land.

Dear God, I will wait on You to make good things happen.
You always do at just the perfect time. Amen.

One Green Leaf

Genesis 8:9-12

The dove came back to the boat. It had not found any place to land. So everyone stayed snuggled inside the boat. They waited. Little by little, the earth began to dry. Noah tried again. He took the dove and set it free. Again, the dove came back. But this time, the dove had a green leaf in its beak. The dove had found land.

Dear God, You have good things planned for me.
I will wait on You during the hard times. Amen.

Boat on a Mountain

Genesis 8:13-19

Thump, went the boat. They had landed on a rock. From there, they could see the water get lower and lower and lower. "It is time," God told Noah. The doors of the boat were opened. Out came the animals. At last, they were on dry land again . . . in a world that was beautiful and new.

Dear God, It is so nice when hard times go away. Thank You that Your love is always there through it all. Amen.

DAY 17

The Animals' Keeper

Genesis 8:20-9:3

It sure felt good to be back on land. Noah got down to pray. God told Noah and his family, "Over every bird and fish and animal, it is people who are in charge. So watch out for the animals and for one another. May your families grow and grow until you fill the whole earth." And so God blessed Noah and his family.

Dear God, You put me and everyone in charge of the earth You made. Help me to take care of it. Amen.

The Promise in a Rainbow

Genesis 9:8-17

God's love was all around them in the fresh buds of spring. Noah lifted his face to the sun with gladness. There in the sky was something no one had ever seen before. Stripes of every lovely color curved over the earth. Had there ever been anything so beautiful? "This is a rainbow," said God. "I made it so that everyone would know this promise that I will never flood the earth again."

Dear God, You make beautiful things just like the rainbow. It helps me to remember Your love. Amen.

The Way to Heaven

Genesis 11:1-4

Beautiful colors shone across the sky. The rainbow showed the people how much God loved them and that He would never again flood the earth. The people just needed to obey God from now on. Then one day, they would meet God in heaven. A few folks got to thinking. Heaven sounded great, but it was not always easy to obey God. Maybe there was an easier way to get to heaven? The people made a plan. They were going to build a tower all the way to heaven so that they could climb up to heaven all by themselves.

Dear God, We can't do anything to be You. You are the only God, and Your plan for us is good. Amen.

DAY 20

The Tower of Babel

Genesis 11:5-9

One brick, two bricks, three bricks, four. The people had begun to build. They were making a tower to reach to heaven. God saw what they were doing. And He did not like it at all. But God had just the way to stop them. The builders stood still in surprise. *What is going on?* they thought. All of a sudden, each person was babbling in a new language. No one could understand what his friends were saying. No one could help each other. No one could build. They took one last, sad look at their tower. Then, everyone went home.

Dear God, When I go the wrong way, sometimes You have to turn me the right way by putting something in my way. Amen.

The Servant Job

Job 1:1-8

Job was the greatest man in all the east. He was very, very rich. He was good, and he was wise. Job had lots of friends and a great big family. Above all, Job loved God. And God loved Job. One day, the devil paid a visit to God. The devil had been spying on the earth, he told God. "Did you see my servant Job?" God asked. "Job turns away from all that is bad. He does only good."

Dear God, I want to be like Job and love You more than anything else. Amen.

Job Is Tested

Job 1:9-17, 20-22

God was proud of what a good servant Job was. "Ha!" said the devil. "Being good is easy when you are rich. But take Job's riches away," said the devil to God, "and then see how much he likes You." "Very well," God told the devil, "you may test him." Job found that all his animals had died in just one day. Now he was poor. Yet—Job did not blame God. He praised God instead. And God was happy.

Dear God, Give me a heart that will praise You when I have a lot and praise You when I have nothing. Amen.

Job Becomes Sick

Job 2:3-10

The devil came again. He said to God, "Of course Job serves You . . . You keep him healthy." God answered, "Very well, let Job be tested." So Job became very sick. He cried out in pain. Job's friends said, "What made God so angry?" But Job knew he had done nothing wrong. And as sick as he was, Job did not blame God. So God was happy with Job still.

Dear God, Help me to praise You and love You
when I am healthy and when I am not. Amen.

DAY 24

Reward for Job

Job 42:10-17

Job had lost almost all his riches and family and health. He felt so sick that he could die. Job's friends only made him feel worse. But even still, Job did not blame God. At last, God answered Job's prayer for help. He made Job all better, and Job leaped with joy. Job became richer than he had ever been before. God gave Job back all that he had lost and more. Job had trusted God even in the bad times.

Dear God, Even though it may take time, You always answer the prayers of Your people. Amen.

On the Road

Genesis 12:1-9

Abraham and Sarah trusted God. So when God said to leave their home and family behind, they left it all. They knew God would keep them safe. Abraham and Sarah now lived in a tent. They did not get sad if others were mean. They could always move their tent somewhere else. But it might be nice to have a real house and to have children. Yet Abraham and Sarah knew that God was taking care of them. So whatever they might miss, they stayed glad. And that made God glad, too.

Dear God, Wherever I go, I feel at home because You are with me. Amen.

DAY 26

A Promise in the Stars

Genesis 15:1-6

It was a night with no clouds in the sky. *The stars have never looked so bright,* Abraham thought. Then, a gentle voice spoke. "Do you see all these stars?" said God. Abraham looked up. Some of the stars sparkled more than others. But each star was like a tiny, glittery jewel. "One day," said God, "your family will be as many as these stars." Abraham looked across the sky with wide eyes. He still did not even have one child, but he trusted God's promise.

Dear God, Even though I am small, You
still have big jobs for me to do. Amen.

DAY 27

Sarah's Wish

Genesis 18:1-14

Sarah had a wish. She wanted a baby. She prayed and she waited. Years went by and still no baby. One day, some visitors came. Sarah was making dinner when one visitor told Abraham that a baby was on its way. Sarah laughed right out loud. Who ever heard of an old lady having a baby? Yet the visitors were from heaven. "Why did Sarah laugh?" said the angel. "Nothing is too hard for God."

Dear God, All that You promise will come true.
Help me to be patient and wait. Amen.

DAY 28

The City of Sin

Genesis 18:20-33; 19:13,27-29

The people in the city were full of sin. God told Abraham, "I will go and see if the people in the city are sorry." If not, then God would destroy it all. Abraham had a big heart. "What about the people who are good?" said Abraham. God answered that if He could find fifty good people there, then the city would be saved. Abraham said, "How about forty?" "Very well," said God, "how about thirty?" said Abraham. "Fine," said God. "How about twenty?" "Twenty then," said God. "How about ten?" said Abraham. "Will You save the city if there are ten good people?" "Yes," said God. He would save it if just ten people were good. But the people were bad, and God had to destroy the city.

Dear God, Your people choose to do good or do wrong, and You punish them when they do wrong. Help me to do right. Amen.

The Child of Promise

Genesis 21:1-7

God always keeps His promises. Sarah knew that now for sure. Her hair might be gray, but Sarah was finally going to have a baby. Little Isaac was born right on time, God's time. Sarah and Abraham were full of love for their tiny son. "Who ever thought," said Sarah, "of two old folks having a baby?" Abraham was more than a hundred years old! "God has made me laugh," Sarah said.

Dear God, I don't always understand Your plans, but they always turn out very good. Amen.

DAY 30

A Test for Abraham

Genesis 22:1-18

Did Abraham love Isaac more than God? It was time to find out. God asked if Abraham would give back his son. Of course, Abraham would. He would do anything that God asked him. So, Abraham took Isaac to the altar. There, Abraham prayed. If God wanted Isaac back, then Abraham would trust him into God's care. Now God knew the truth, that Abraham put God first. This made God happy. Abraham found a ram caught in the bushes nearby, and God told him to put the ram on the altar instead. So Isaac went back home with his father.

Dear God, You might ask me to do something that is hard. Help me to be strong to do the right thing. Amen.

DAY 31

Rebekah at the Well

Genesis 24:1-21

"Please God," prayed the servant, "help me find the right wife for Isaac." Then he headed off by camel. Rebekah was on her way to the well. She could see a group of camels up ahead. The servant prayed, "God, if one of the girls who come to the well for water offers me and my camels something to drink, I will know she is the wife for Isaac." Rebekah filled her pitcher with water. "Please, drink," she said to the man with the camels. Then Rebekah gave water to his camels as well. The servant simply smiled. He knew that God had answered his prayer.

Dear God, Help me to be kind to everyone I meet and show them Your love. Amen.

Kind Rebekah

Genesis 24:22-51

Rebekah was beautiful and kind. Yet . . . the servant only wanted a wife for Isaac who was from their land, too. The servant gave her a gold earring and bracelets he had brought as presents. "Where are you from?" he asked a bit nervously. Rebekah said she was from their land! Now the servant just had to find out if she and her family would agree to a wedding. Over supper that night, the servant told her parents all about how he had found Rebekah. "This is of God," they said. "Yes, she may marry Isaac."

Dear God, You have good surprises waiting for me. Help me to trust You and wait for them. Amen.

DAY 33

Rebekah and Isaac

Genesis 24:57-67

Rebekah's parents had a question. Was she ready to get married? Rebekah did not have to think long. The answer was yes. So she said her goodbyes. Then Rebekah went with the servant on the back of a camel. After traveling a long way, the camel train crossed a field where Isaac was sitting. He looked up and saw Rebekah, the loveliest lady. The two were married right away. Rebekah and Isaac would love each other forever and always.

Dear God, You are always there to help me do the right thing. Help me to know where You want me to go. Amen.

DAY 34

Rebekah Talks with God

Genesis 25:21-23

Rebekah's belly was big and round. The baby kicked and kicked. Was something wrong? She prayed to God for help. God had an answer. Rebekah was not just having one baby . . . she was having twins! They would each grow up to be strong, God told her. They would each start a new nation of their own. Rebekah smiled. God never stops giving wonderful gifts.

Dear God, When I am worried, I will tell You about it. You can answer all my questions as I grow. Amen.

Two Baby Boys

Genesis 25:24-34

Isaac and Rebekah had twins. Esau was born first. That meant he would get their father's lands. Esau had the birthright. One day, Esau came in from the field starving. He was so hungry he could faint. "Quick," Esau said to his brother Jacob, "give me some stew." Jacob thought it over. "How about a trade?" said Jacob. "Some stew for your birthright." Esau thought, *who cares who was born first?* He agreed to the trade. Then Esau gobbled down his stew.

Dear God, Thank You for giving me talents of my own. These are all gifts from You. Amen.

DAY 36

Farmer Isaac

Genesis 26:12-31

God was good to Isaac and Rebekah. The farm grew, and they became rich. But their neighbors got jealous. They sent the family away. Isaac and Rebekah would have to start a new farm from scratch. Isaac began to dig a well. Just then, he spotted his old neighbors. Had they come to make trouble? Not at all. They said, "We can see God loves your family very much, and we are sorry for sending you away. Let's stay friends and treat each other well." To this Isaac agreed.

Dear God, Help me to trust You when bad things happen
and to show others You are trustworthy too. Amen.

Isaac's Gift

Genesis 27:1-29

Many years went by. Isaac could now hardly see. It was time to pass along what was his. So Isaac called for Esau, but Jacob came instead. After all, he and Esau had made a deal. He had traded Esau soup for getting the birthright. Isaac heard someone at the door. "Is that you, Esau?" said his father. Jacob lied. "Yes, Father," said Jacob. Isaac reached out his hands. All that he had would now be for his son. "And may God," said Isaac, "make you great." Then he sealed it with a kiss on Jacob's head.

Dear God, Your plans cannot be stopped. I know that You are in control, and You always do good things. Amen.

Jacob Pays a Price

Genesis 27:30-45

Esau had heard Isaac wanted to see him. "Here I am, Father," said Esau. Yet Esau had come too late. Isaac had given all he had to Jacob. Esau was so mad he could cry. It just wasn't fair. Jacob was getting everything. Esau was getting nothing. He would make his brother pay, alright, for such a mean trick! Rebekah said that it might be best for Jacob to go away for a bit, just until Esau had calmed down. So Jacob hit the road on his own.

Dear God, When things don't seem fair, help me to trust You to make it better. Amen.

A Rock for a Pillow

Genesis 28:10-15

It was growing dark. Time to get some rest. But Jacob was out in nature and far from any bed. So Jacob laid his head down on a rock instead. Then he shut his eyes. Jacob began to dream. He saw stairs reaching up, up, up all the way to Heaven. Angels were going up and down it. At the very top was God. And God had some news. Jacob would have a big family one day, God told him. And they would all live on the very land where Jacob was sleeping. "I will be with you always," said God.

Dear God, You sometimes talk to people in dreams. Help me to listen as You talk to me. Amen.

Love for Rachel

Genesis 29:1-11

Jacob walked, and he walked. He came to some sheep lying beside a water well. "Why not give your sheep a drink?" said Jacob to the shepherds. They pointed to the big rock over the well. That's when Jacob saw her. The loveliest lady was coming down the road. She was bringing sheep to the well herself. Jacob reached out for the rock and pushed with all his might. Away the rock tumbled. Jacob had saved the day. And he had found his true love as well. It was Rachel . . . the woman who cared for the sheep.

Dear God, When I feel alone, You are
always there to lead me. Amen.

DAY 41

Animals for Jacob

Genesis 30:27-43

Rachel's father was rich, and he was crafty. He saw that Jacob got help from God. "Work for me," said Rachel's father. "I will pay you whatever you want." "Very well," said Jacob. He wanted animals as pay. Jacob would get to keep all of the animals with spots. Pay day came at last. Jacob went out to the field. He could hardly believe his eyes—all the strongest animals now had spots. Suddenly Jacob had more goats, sheep, and cows than his boss. Jacob now was a very wealthy guy.

Dear God, Thank You for giving me good things. You make my life wonderful. Amen.

Two Sisters Choose

Genesis 31:3-18

Jacob now had his own big family. Still, he missed his mother and father. Jacob went to talk to Rachel and her sister, Leah. Would they go with Jacob back to his own land? The two sisters thought it over. They had seen their father be mean to Jacob even though Jacob worked hard. So, Rachel and Leah said yes. They waited until their father wasn't looking. Then, they took their children and snuck away with Jacob.

Dear God, When someone is mean to me, help me to show them Your love. Amen.

DAY 43

The Name of Israel

Genesis 32:24-30

It was dark when Jacob saw the man standing right in his way. In a flash, the two were wrestling. They tumbled, and they rolled. At last, the stranger cried out. "Let me go," he said. "The sun is coming up." Jacob answered, "First, bless me." The man agreed. "I will give you a new name," he said. "From now on you will be called Israel." Jacob was amazed. The word "Israel" meant "wrestles with God." Who was this man? Jacob wanted to know. But the stranger didn't tell him. Instead he blessed Jacob, who was to be called Israel. Now Jacob knew . . . that he had wrestled with the Lord.

Dear God, I can always ask You when I don't understand something. You are always with me. Amen.

DAY 44

Two Brothers

Genesis 33:1-7

The family had traveled a long, long way. When Jacob looked up—he froze. It was his brother, Esau! Was Esau still angry over Jacob's trick? Esau ran up to Jacob. Yet instead of fighting, Esau kissed him. Both brothers cried for joy to see each other again. Esau asked, "Who are all these people?" Jacob smiled proudly. He called his family over to meet his big brother.

Dear God, Thank You for being a forgiving God and for teaching me to forgive, too. Amen.

DAY 45

The Colorful Coat

Genesis 37:1-4

Jacob had twelve fine sons. Next to last was Joseph. One day, Jacob called to Joseph. Jacob had a present for his son. It was a coat, a wonderful coat of many colors. The coat made his brothers feel angry. Why did only Joseph get a coat? Joseph tried not to mind their mean looks. He could see his father loved him very much. What a fancy coat it was indeed!

Dear God, Thank You that I am special to You
and that You care for me. Amen.

Joseph Has a Dream

Genesis 37:5-11

When Joseph was growing up, he sometimes heard God speak to him in his dreams. One morning, Joseph burst out of bed. He ran to tell his family what he dreamed. "One day you will all come and bow to me, and I will be your ruler," Joseph said. "And all of you, my servants." His brothers glared back. "Dream on, kid," they said. Then they went on with their work, hating Joseph even more. And they did not worry about the words of their silly little brother.

Dear God, You have a special plan for me even
though I am small. Teach me to listen to You. Amen.

A Wicked Plan

Genesis 37:19-28

The brothers had grown sick of hearing Joseph act so proud. They stuck him in a pit. Now they did not have to listen to his chatter anymore. Just then, some travelers were going by on their way to Egypt. His brothers pulled Joseph out of the pit. Did the travelers have room for a pesky little brother?

Dear God, If I am scared or if someone treats me mean, help me know that You are here and will save me. Amen.

A Far Away Land

Genesis 39:1

So this was Egypt. To Joseph, every sight and sound was new and strange. Poor Joseph had lost it all. His brothers had sent him far from home. Joseph missed his father very much. Even the special coat was gone. Yet Joseph decided to be brave. He knew that God would be with him. And Joseph was right. Soon he got a job. Joseph would be a servant to someone rich and important.

Dear God, I trust You to do good things in my life even when I don't understand. Amen.

DAY 49

The Glad Servant

Genesis 39:2-6

The rich man smiled. This new servant, Joseph, sure was a hard worker. He always told the truth as well. And all that Joseph did worked out great. His boss could see that God was with Joseph. So, he put Joseph in charge. The rich man made Joseph the top servant in the house. If others needed this or that, it would be Joseph who held the keys.

Dear God, I will always do my best in
everything because I love You. Amen.

DAY 50

A Cruel Trick

Genesis 39:7-19

The lady of the house had started playing tricks. Joseph tried his best to stay away. But things just got worse and worse. One day, she went to see the boss. "Look," said the lady. "Here is a piece of Joseph's robe. I caught him when he snuck into my room." She lied to get Joseph in trouble. But Joseph knew God could always make things right.

Dear God, Some people may try to hurt my feelings. Help me to know that You love me and are with me. Amen.

God's Good Care

Genesis 39:20-40:15

The lady of the house had told a lie. And the rich man had believed her. So Joseph was sent away once again but this time, straight to jail. Joseph stayed brave. God was with him even in jail. Joseph did not sit around feeling sad. He would help the others in the jail. When they had a dream they did not understand, Joseph would help, telling them what it meant.

Dear God, Whenever I'm not in a nice place and I'm having a hard time, help me to see what good I can do. Amen.

DAY 52

Joseph and the King

Genesis 41:1-36

The king was feeling glum. He had dreamed a funny dream, and no one could tell him what it meant. Just then, the cupbearer spoke up. There was a man in the jail who knew about dreams. *Creak* went the jail door. Joseph found himself in front of the king. Did Joseph know what the dream meant? Joseph stood up tall. "Your dream," said Joseph to the king, "means the land will all dry up, so you need to save up food."

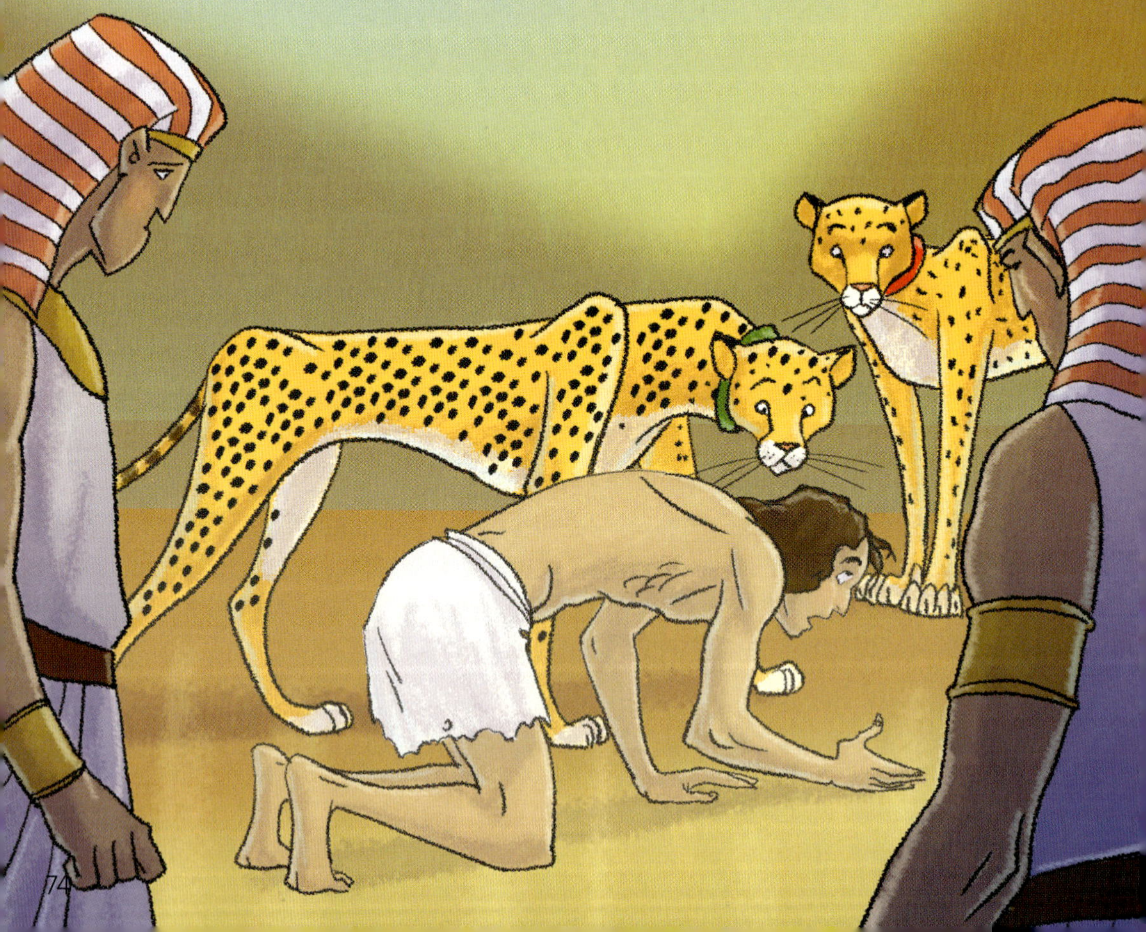

Dear God, You might sometimes allow hard things to come to help me understand how to be nice to others. Amen.

A Ruler Is Made

Genesis 41:37-45

The king had been given some news, some really big news. The water was going to dry up. But thanks to Joseph, they had time to get ready. The king could have *hugged* Joseph! He took off his kingly ring. He put it on Joseph's finger. No more jail for Joseph. The king was putting him in charge. Joseph would now be a very important person. No one, except for the king, would be as important as Joseph.

Dear God, You make all things right. You lift me up when I am feeling sad. Amen.

Seven Good Years

Genesis 41:46-52

Joseph was now the boss. He told the people what to do with the crops. He stored it in cities around the country. There was so much in storage that Joseph stopped counting. And soon enough, the water dried up . . . just like Joseph had told the king. But in Egypt, all would be well. Joseph had made sure of that. There were piles and piles of food saved up. Soon many countries came to Egypt for food. But since God had warned Joseph, he was able to help them all with the food he had saved.

Dear God, You put people in charge and make people smart. It is You who does all these things. Amen.

DAY 55

The Visitors

Genesis 42:1-14

The palace had visitors. Some men from far away wanted to buy food. Would his majesty share just a pinch? The men wanted to know. Joseph looked at the men. These were his brothers! Every one of them was there —except for Benjamin, Joseph's only little brother. He felt so happy he could cry. But—should Joseph help them? They had not been very nice, after all. Of course Joseph would help. But first, he would test them to find out if they had gotten rid of Benjamin just like they once tried to get rid of him. "I think you are *spies!*" Joseph told the brothers. "So I am keeping you here."

Dear God, You make wonderful things
happen to me and to others. Amen.

DAY 56

The Youngest Brother

Genesis 42:15-43:15

Benjamin had stayed at home. And Joseph wanted to see his little brother very much. So he ordered someone to go and get him. The brothers felt afraid. What was this ruler going to do to them? They still did not see that it was Joseph. "It was all *your* idea to hurt Joseph," said one brother to the rest. "Now God is punishing us!" The brothers packed their donkeys to go get Benjamin. *At least*, they thought, *we were able to buy food for father.*

Dear God, When I am angry, help me not to do anything mean but instead to ask You to help me. Amen.

Joseph's Secret

Genesis 45:1-15

Joseph burst with joy when he saw his little brother. Benjamin just stared back. "Why had the ruler begun to cry?" the boy wondered. The older brothers were not sure *what* to think. Then, the ruler called them over. He was ready to tell the truth. He was Joseph, their own little brother.

DAY 57

Dear God, When I give my anger to You, I feel much better. Amen.

DAY 58

The Family Together

Genesis 46:29-47:12

Joseph forgave his brothers. He asked them to come and live in the best part of Egypt, a place called Goshen. Their father could come along too, of course. So the family packed up and moved to Egypt. They would all be back together again in a land where Joseph was like a king with plenty of food and gladness as long as they lived.

Dear God, You give us so many good things,
more than we can even imagine. Amen.

DAY 59

A Land Gone Bad

Exodus 1:1-14

Many years later after Joseph had died, the family of Israel grew and grew. It made the new Egyptian king worry. What if this family tried to take charge? The king made a plan. He would make them all be slaves. Now the people of Israel could not get high and mighty. They would work hard all day long—or else. The sun was hot. The guards were mean. The slaves prayed to God for help. And God, of course, was listening.

Dear God, When I am in trouble,
I will come to You. Amen.

A Baby in a Basket

Exodus 2:1-6

Miriam loved her baby brother. She wanted him safe from the wicked king. When Moses' mother put him in a basket in the river, Miriam watched him closely. Then— along came the princess to take her bath. Miriam sent the basket down the river. "Look!" cried the princess. "A baby in a basket. I think I will adopt him," she said. Miriam's plan had worked! No one would harm the baby of a princess.

Dear God, I want my words and actions to be part of Your plans. Amen.

DAY 61

Prince Moses

Exodus 2:7-10

There came a tiny voice from the grass. It was Miriam. She had an idea to help the princess. "I know a good nanny," said Miriam. The princess thought Miriam was a nice little girl. Miriam ran straight home to get their mom who would get to take care of Moses. He was a baby who would now grow up as a prince.

Dear God, You are watching over everyone. You
work everything out in amazing ways. Amen.

DAY 62

The Runaway

Exodus 2:11-20

Moses was all grown up, but the king didn't want him there anymore. So Moses ran far away. At last, he rested. What was he going to do now? Some sisters came along to water their sheep. Moses was kind. He helped the sisters water their sheep. "We met the nicest young man," the sisters told their father. Moses soon became part of their family.

Dear God, When I feel I don't have a friend, You make my heart feel better. I trust You to bring me a good friend. Amen.

DAY 63

The Burning Bush

Exodus 3:1-14

Moses was looking after the sheep when all of a sudden, a bush burst into fire! It was God telling Moses to listen up. "Go back to the palace," said God. He wanted Moses to free the Israelites from their slavery. Moses was not so sure. The king would not listen to anyone. Not to Moses . . . no even to God. Yet God told Moses not to worry. "I will go with you," said God.

Dear God, Even when I don't understand your plan, I will say yes to doing what You ask me to do. Amen.

DAY 64

The Walking Stick

Exodus 4:1-5

Moses was worried. Would the Israelites believe that God had sent him? God had a plan for that, too. He told Moses to throw down his staff. Moses jumped away because the stick had turned into a snake! It wriggled and wiggled on the ground below. God said, "Now grab it by the tail." Moses reached out. The snake turned back into wood. The slaves would trust in Moses alright. He just had to show them this miracle.

Dear God, I don't feel strong enough to do anything for You. Help me to know it is You who makes me strong. Amen.

A Brother for a Helper

Exodus 4:10-17

There was one more thing. Moses did not feel he was good at speaking. Very well then. God said that Moses would have a helper. His brother Aaron was good at speaking, so Aaron would be the one doing the talking. As a matter of fact, Aaron was already on his way to meet with Moses. He would be very glad to see his brother again.

Dear God, Even when I am not sure about everything, I still believe in You. Help me to have a pure heart. Amen.

DAY 66

The Prince Returns

Exodus 4:20-31

Moses did all that God had said. He went to Egypt. He got all the Israelite leaders in one place. Moses told them that God had heard them ask for help. And now God was going to do something about it. The people of Israel were filled with joy. God had sent a leader to set them free! God had not forgotten them. He had come to the rescue right on time.

Dear God, I know You hear my prayers. Thank You for always hearing me and coming to the rescue. Amen.

DAY 67

Face to Face

Exodus 5:1-5

It could not wait any longer. The people of Israel were hurting. It was time for Moses to face the king. The king did not look glad to see him. But Moses did his best to be brave. God had a message, so Moses told the king, "Let my people go." But the king only laughed. "No one tells me what to do," said the king. "Why should I take orders from God?"

Dear God, Protect me from evil and help me to be courageous. Amen.

The King Gets a Lesson

Exodus 5:6-6:11; 7:10-24

Things were not going well. Moses had told the slaves that he had come to help. But instead, things got worse. Moses had made the king mad. So now the slaves had to work even more. And their guards were meaner than ever. God said to wait and to trust. Soon enough, God taught the king a lesson. When the Egyptian people went to the river for water, the water had turned into blood.

Dear God, When others don't do right, I won't fight but will leave it up to You. Amen.

DAY 69

Land of Frogs

Exodus 8:1-15

The water smelled like rotten fish. Across the land, people pinched their noses. Moses said again, "Let my people go." "No way!" said the king. "Very well," Moses told him. The king would be punished. And God did just that with frogs from out of the sky. Soon, frogs were in every nook and cranny. There were frogs in the ovens and frogs in the beds. All of Egypt had become filled with frogs.

Dear God, When I am afraid, I will remember that
You are in control and You will give me peace. Amen.

Itching and Buzzing

Exodus 8:15-32

The king was not going to free the slaves over some silly frogs. So God would punish him again. The people all started to itch with lice. But the king would not listen just because of lice. "Let them go," Moses said, "or else." The king did not budge. So clouds of flies came in filling up the palace. Every street was soon abuzz with pesky flies.

Dear God, Whatever hard thing comes, I will look to You for my strength and happiness. Amen.

DAY 71

The Cows and Boils

Exodus 9-10:20

His cows had all died. The king growled, full of fury. He was not letting those slaves go after this! Not now and not ever. Before long, the Egyptians all got sick. Yet the king would still not free the slaves. So God sent a hailstorm then giant locusts. At last the people of Egypt had enough. "Please," they begged their king, "just let those people *go*."

Dear God, When I am sad or in trouble, please come help me do what is right. Amen.

DAY 72

Darkness on Egypt

Exodus 10:21-12:32

The king did not care what anyone had to say. So God sent darkness. The whole sky over Egypt went black. Moses gave the king one last warning. But the king did not listen, and when he woke up, his son had died. Now the king had enough. "Get out of here, Moses!" he cried. "And take those slaves with you." The people of Israel were finally free.

Dear God, Waiting and waiting is hard
to do. Help me to be patient. Amen.

DAY 73

The Exodus

Exodus 12:33-14:2

The people of Israel got ready in a hurry. They called their animals and packed as fast as they could. They would be gone before the sun had even come up. God showed them where to go using a tall cloud in the sky. They rested when they got to the sea. It was time to thank God. God had heard their prayers and set them free.

Dear God, Like the beautiful sunrise, You want to make my
heart beautiful too. And that makes me so happy! Amen.

DAY 74

The Chase

Exodus 14:5-22

The Israelites were camping by the seaside when they looked up and could hardly believe what they saw. There was the whole Egyptian army coming after them! Pharaoh had decided to get his slaves back after all. But Moses had faith. He reached out his staff over the sea, and there the waves started to peel back on either side. The sea had split in two. A path of land had appeared. The Israelites hurried to safety on the other side of the sea.

Dear God, You are my Savior, and You will rescue me. Amen.

Song of Miriam

Exodus 15:19-21

The people were safe at last! It was time to thank God. It was time to make music and to dance. Miriam the prophetess led them in a song of joy. "Sing to God," she sang. "God has won out over all!"

DAY 76

Bread from Heaven

Exodus 16:2-18

The people were hungry. "If only we were still slaves," they whined, "then at least we would not starve." Moses prayed to God for help. The next morning thin flakes like bread had fallen from Heaven. God had sent them food to eat. And the people went out to pick up the bread with thankful hearts.

Dear God, You are ready to help me when I have a need. You even made bread appear on the ground! Amen.

A Desert Place

Exodus 17:1-7

"We are thirsty," cried the people. "Give us water." Moses told them, "Why do you complain? Why don't you trust in God?" Then Moses prayed. God answered and told Moses just what to do. Moses went to the rock that God had said. He gave it a good *whack* with his staff. Then, out of the rock came the water gushing cool and clear.

Dear God, Whatever You ask me to do, You will bring me all that I need to do it. Amen.

DAY 78

Moses and the Law

Exodus 19:3-25

God called Moses up to the mountain top. God was going to give Moses the Law. From the ground below, the people saw a cloud swallow the mountain. Was Moses going to be okay? But down came Moses again, perfectly fine. "God was talking to Moses on that mountain," said the people. So they listened to all that Moses had heard from God.

Dear God, Please give me what I need to tell people
about You so they will listen and believe in You. Amen

DAY 79

Ten Commandments

Exodus 20:1-21

God gave Moses ten laws on stone tablets. "There will be no gods but Me," God said. He did not want the people praying to other gods. He wanted them to love others, to not use curse words, and to keep one day a week as holy. They must not kill, or cheat, or steal. They must not lie or wish for what was not theirs. The people had seen the mountain shake when God was giving Moses the Law. "Don't be afraid," Moses told them. God had given them laws in order to help them.

Dear God, You give me rules to keep me safe
and happy. Help me to obey You. Amen.

DAY 80

The Tabernacle

Exodus 25:1-22

It was time to build a special house for God, a place to give God thanks, a place to put things that were very precious—like the stone tablets. God had told Moses just how to make it . . . with curtains of blue, and purple, and red, and with gold carvings of flowers and angels. Each person in the camp gave what felt right in his own heart. Some gave gold or silver. Some gave their talents like making fancy cloth. When they had made the house, they made an ark of gold to put the tablets in.

Dear God, You give me so much. I want to give You what I have because I love You. Amen.

Joshua Leads the People

Joshua 1:1-9

The desert was hot and dusty. The Israelites wanted to leave, but they waited on God. At last, God said it was time. Moses had died, and Joshua was the new leader. "Be strong," God told Joshua, "and be brave." Joshua was going to lead the people into their new land.

Dear God, Help me to be strong and brave. I believe in You. Amen.

The Spies of Joshua

Joshua 2:2-21

There were soldiers at the door. They wanted to know where Joshua's spies were. "Sorry," said Rahab "there are no spies in *this* house." But Rahab had hidden the two spies. She knew that God loved them, so she would help them escape. The spies said they would protect Rahab and her family. Then they climbed down a rope from the window.

Dear God, Help me to know what is right and true. Amen.

A Land of Their Own

Joshua 2:24-3:17

Across the river, the people jumped for joy. They were done living in the desert. Here it was green and beautiful. This was the land God had said He would give them: a land of milk and honey, a land they could call their very own. God stopped the river, and they crossed over on dry land to their new home.

Dear God, All good things come from You. I will be patient for You to give to me what I need. Amen.

DAY 84

The Fall of Jericho

Joshua 6:1-20

Jericho was a city behind a high, strong wall. But no wall can keep out God. And God had decided to give the city to the people of Israel. God told their leader Joshua just what to do. Joshua marched the Israelites around the city. Around and around and around they went. They blew on their trumpets. Each gave a shout. Then as they watched, the walls of Jericho fell!

Dear God, Just trumpets can't break a wall, but You showed the people that You are strong and in charge. Amen.

DAY 85

The Sun and Moon Obey

Joshua 10:5-14

Joshua had to keep fighting other enemies that were so big and strong. Yet God said not to be afraid. He promised to help the people win. So Joshua felt brave and believed. He was not giving up. "Sun and moon," said Joshua, "stay right where you are!" And the sun and the moon obeyed. They stayed right where they were until Joshua's people had won the fight.

Dear God, You help me be brave and strong. I believe that You can do anything. Amen.

Land for All

Joshua 13:1-33

The people had once been slaves. But now, God's promise was coming true. They were winning their own land, city by city. The new land would be called Israel. Joshua made sure that each tribe got a fair share of the new land. Many years later, their capital would be Jerusalem, the holy city. God's promises had finally come true.

Dear God, Your promises always come true. I will remember what good things You have done. Amen.

Judge Deborah

Judges 4:1-9

Deborah was the judge over all of Israel. A cruel general named Sisera had come to the land. Deborah told her soldiers to go and fight him. She promised that God was going to help them win. The soldiers were afraid of General Sisera's weapons. They begged Deborah, "Please come with us!" Deborah was not afraid. "Very well," she answered, "then God will give the victory to a woman."

Dear God, Help me to stand up tall and do good when You give me a job to do. Amen.

DAY 88

Deborah's Victory

Judges 4:10-16

Deborah stood and went with the army. General Sisera heard that they were coming. He got his weapons ready. Deborah told her soldiers, "Up! God is with you." The general was suddenly afraid. He ran away as fast as his feet could go. That was the end of any trouble from General Sisera. Deborah's people could now rest safe and sound.

Dear God, Sometimes You let me have hard times so I will need You to make me brave. I know You will stay beside me. Amen.

Jael the Brave

Judges 4:17-22

The rotten general ran from Deborah's army, fast and far. "Hide here," said Jael. She gave the general some milk to drink. Yet Jael knew just how awful this man really was. When Deborah's army came by, she called them in. "I have who you are looking for," said Jael.

Dear God, Help me to obey You
even when it is hard. Amen.

Deborah Sings of Jael

Judges 5:24-31

"Great is Jael!" sang Deborah. "She was not afraid to help your people get rid of their enemies. May all your enemies, Lord, disappear too. But may those who love you be strong and bright like the sun."

Dear God, Help me be a hero for You and do what is right even when it is hard. Amen.

The Angel and Gideon

Judges 6:11-16

"God is with you," said the angel, "oh brave and mighty one." Gideon had been pounding wheat when he saw someone under a tree. The angel said that Gideon was going to save his land and the people of Israel from their enemies. There had to be some mistake. Gideon had no way to save the land, he told the angel nicely. After all, he was only a poor farmer. Yet the angel said that it was Gideon God had picked alright. Gideon would save the land without a big army to help him.

Dear God, You don't look on the outside, but You look at my heart. Make my heart lovely like Yours. Amen.

DAY 92

The Broken Statue

Judges 6:25-31

It was time to make a move. Gideon was still a bit afraid though. So he snuck out into the night when no one would see. The next day, the city was in an uproar. Gideon had cut down the statue that they prayed to. Gideon's father stood up for his son and kept him safe. "If the statue is really a god," said Gideon's dad, "then let it stand up for itself."

Gideon Wants to be Sure

Judges 6:36-40

Gideon was still not sure. Would God please give him a sign? A sign to make Gideon sure that God really had picked him to help his people. Gideon laid some wool down on the floor. The next morning, the wool was all wet while the ground was perfectly dry! It seemed like magic. Still, Gideon wanted to be extra, *extra* sure. Would God please switch them the next day? Sure enough, the wool kept dry while the ground got wet. *Okay then,* thought Gideon, *God wanted a farm boy to be a warrior.*

Dear God, You made me special like no one else, and You have a special plan for me. Amen.

DAY 94

A Warrior for God

Judges 7:1-25; 8:22-23

Gideon was ready to go and fight for God. "Not so fast," God said because he wanted the people to know that God was the one in charge. So God told Gideon to send most of his soldiers home. Then with just a tiny army, Gideon led them to battle, and God helped them win. Afterwards, the people begged Gideon to be their king. But Gideon said, "It is God who shall be your King."

Dear God, When other people praise me, I will tell them 'thank you' and that it was You who helped me. Amen.

DAY 95

Samson the Strong

Judges 13:1-24

An angel told a woman she would have a son. When the baby came, his mother named him Samson. She was careful to obey all the angel told her to do. She fed Samson good, clean foods, but most importantly, she made sure to never cut his hair. Samson was blessed and grew big and strong and brave.

Dear God, The angels are Your messengers, and
You sent them to tell Your good news. Amen.

Samson and the Lion

Judges 14:5-7

Samson went for a walk one day. Suddenly—there stood a lion roaring right at him! Samson had no weapons to help him. But Samson was not afraid. God was there. Samson killed the lion using just his hands. Then he went on his way to find his parents. Yet Samson never bragged to anyone about what a mighty thing that he had done.

Dear God, You are the one who makes people strong and brave. Amen.

Delilah's Trick

Judges 16:4-20

Samson punished his enemies with his strength. Wherever Samson went, people shook with fear. Samson's enemies asked his girlfriend, Delilah, to find out the secret to his strength. Delilah begged, "Why are you so strong?" Samson told her at last, "I must never cut my hair." That night, Samson's hair was cut while he slept. Samson awoke. Why had he trusted Delilah? His hair was now short. His strength was no more.

Dear God, Help me not to be selfish and brag about myself. Help me be humble and put others first. Amen.

DAY 98

Samson's Last Stand

Judges 16:20-30

Samson had been tricked. He had shared his secret. And now he was in jail without the power to escape. One evening when Samson's enemies where celebrating their false god, they told the guards, "Let's laugh at the man we once feared." So Samson was taken to the temple in his chains. Yet little did they notice—Samson's hair had grown. Samson prayed to God, "May I have one last chance to be strong." Then Samson pushed the pillars and the temple fell to dust.

Dear God, You will always be near me
when I call to You, no matter what. Amen.

DAY 99

Ruth, the Good Servant

Ruth 1:1-2:18

Ruth lived in a foreign country. Her husband was from Israel, God's chosen people. When he died, his mother, Naomi, told Ruth to go back to her home and her family. But Ruth was not going to leave old Naomi by herself. Ruth went with Naomi back to Israel and worked hard to help Naomi. She picked up scraps of grain in a field for them to eat and barely rested at all. The owner of the field heard of Ruth's good deeds. After that, there was always free grain left for Ruth.

Dear God, You plan what will happen before it ever does. I will trust that Your plan is good. Amen.

DAY 100

Ruth's New Beginning

Ruth 3:1-11, 4:9-17

Ruth had taken good care of Naomi. Naomi wanted Ruth to be cared for, too. She told Ruth, "The owner of the field likes you. Go and visit him." Ruth went to visit Boaz, the owner of the field. It wasn't long before Ruth and Boaz were married. God blessed Ruth with a new family of her own because she had served Him by loving others.

Dear God, Ruth believed in You and trusted You to take care of her, and You did! Amen.

Hannah's Wish

1 Samuel 1:6-28

Hannah cried and cried. She did not want to eat. What she wanted was a child, but a child never came. Hannah prayed, "God, if You give me a child, then I promise the child will be a special gift to You." God heard Hannah's wish. Soon, baby Samuel was born. Hannah remembered always the promise she made to God. When Samuel grew older, she took him to the temple. Happily, Hannah said, "May my child forever serve in the house of God."

Dear God, You always hear my prayers. Help me to trust that You will answer. Amen.

DAY 102

Hannah Sings to God

1 Samuel 2:1-10

"Those who fell," sang Hannah, "God has now made strong. Those who were hungry, God has filled. Those who had no children, now have had their own. God brings down what is bad. God lifts up the good!"

Dear God, It makes You happy to give Your children good things. I am so thankful that You do! Amen.

A Call in the Night

1 Samuel 3:1-10

Samuel heard a voice calling his name. Samuel ran to where the priest was sleeping. "Yes, Master?" said Samuel. The priest gave the boy a funny look. "I did not call you," said Eli. "Go back to bed." Samuel obeyed. But before long, the voice came again. Samuel ran to Eli. "Yes, Master?" Eli at last knew what was going on. He told Samuel just what to do. Samuel went back to bed. When the voice came again, Samuel did not move. He opened his mouth instead. "Yes, God?" said Samuel. "Your servant is listening."

Dear God, Just like Samuel listened to You, help me to hear You and listen to what You say. Amen.

DAY 104

The Prophet

1 Samuel 3:19-8:22

When Samuel was all grown, he was called a prophet. Samuel could hear the voice of God when God spoke. It was Samuel's job to tell the people what God said. It was his job to tell God what the people said as well. The Israelites were not feeling safe. They complained, "We want more than just God. We also want a king." So Samuel the prophet went to speak with God. "Very well," God answered, "I will give them a king."

Dear God, Help me to serve
others and to help them. Amen.

DAY 105

The Lost Donkeys

1 Samuel 9:2-10:1

Saul was looking for his donkeys when he met Samuel. The prophet knew that this young man was God's choice. Samuel said, "Your donkeys are found; worry no more. Come eat with me." The best seat was made ready for Saul. Saul could hardly believe he was eating with Samuel. Samuel was a prophet while Saul was just a regular young man. When they had eaten, Samuel prayed for Saul and blessed him. Then Samuel said, "God has picked you as the king for His people."

Dear God, I want to serve You, so help me do Your will. Amen.

Time for a King

1 Samuel 10:17-24

It was time for the prophet Samuel to show Israel their king, so Samuel gathered the people together. Then Samuel called out, "Look—there is God's choice! Can you see that he stands high above everyone else?" There, where Samuel was pointing, stood Saul. As the tallest young man in Israel, Saul stuck out of the crowd. Everyone turned to look up at tall Saul. Then all the people cried out, "God save the king!"

Dear God, I will do what You ask me to do and go where You lead me. Amen.

DAY 107

The Young King

1 Samuel 10:27-11:13

Not everyone was excited about their new king. "How will *he* save us from our enemies?" they said. But Saul kept his head high and held his peace. Soon enough, he got his chance to prove himself at war. Saul and his new army beat the enemy . . . in one day! The people cried, "Who said Saul should not be king? Let's get rid of them." But King Saul shook his head no. "For today," he said, "God saved us from our enemy."

Dear God, You choose the leaders, and no
one can change what You have done. Amen.

DAY 108

Sin of Saul

1 Samuel 13:5-14

The Philistine army was huge with horses and chariots. They came closer and closer. Israel's army grew afraid. Some of the soldiers ran off to hide in caves or bushes. Worst of all, Samuel had not yet come to do the blessing. King Saul was worried. He gave up waiting for Samuel and decided he would do the prophet's job himself. Then Samuel arrived. "What have you done?" he said. "God is now going to make someone else the king."

Dear God, Help me not to be too proud, and remind me to honor You first. Amen.

The Shepherd

1 Samuel 16:1-13

The prophet Samuel visited Jesse in Bethlehem. God had chosen one of his sons to be king. Jesse was excited and called in his big, strong sons. Samuel looked them over and asked, "Are these all of your sons?" Jesse said, "Only David, who is watching the sheep, is left. But he's just a boy." Still, Samuel called for David. When Samuel saw the shepherd boy, he said, "He's the one!" Samuel gave David the blessing of a future king.

Dear God, Sometimes I feel too little to do things, but sometimes You choose the littlest to do big jobs. Amen.

DAY 110

A Boy and Harp

1 Samuel 16:14-23

Saul had gone against God. Now he had no more peace. The servants saw their king was unhappy. They said, "Let us bring you a musician to make you feel better." Saul answered, "Very well, whatever you think will help."

The servants heard Jesse had a son good at playing the harp. They brought the youngest son of Jesse to the king. As David played and sang, Saul felt better right away. So David stayed to make his music for the king.

Dear God, I will try hard in all I do because
I want to make You proud. Amen.

The Giant

1 Samuel 17:4-27

David's father told David to take his older brothers their lunch. So the shepherd boy went to where the soldiers were fighting. David arrived at the battlefield as a war cry rang out. He rushed to find his brothers among Israel's army. His brothers and all the soldiers looked terrified. The enemy had a giant named Goliath on their side! But David was not afraid. The boy said, "With our trust in God, why should we be afraid?"

Dear God, Help me to be brave since I know nothing is too big for You. Amen.

The King and David

1 Samuel 17:28-37

David's oldest brother said, "You naughty boy! You left your sheep just so you could see the battle." But Saul did not feel the same way about David. The king wanted to hear what David had to say. David told King Saul, "I will fight Goliath, the giant." "But—" Saul answered, "you're only a boy!" David said, "When taking care of the sheep, I have killed lions and bears. Now with God's help, I will kill Goliath, too."

Dear God, When others think I am too small, I will still do my best. Amen.

DAY 113

David and Goliath

1 Samuel 17:38-49

King Saul gave David a helmet, armor, and a sword. They were all too big and heavy for a boy though. So instead, David picked up five stones to fight with. Then with his slingshot in hand, David met the giant. Goliath glared down. He growled a ferocious growl. David picked a stone from his bag and spun his sling. KA-POW—the stone hit Goliath right in the head! The giant fell face down in the dirt. David had won.

Dear God, When I have a big problem, I will
ask You for the strength to solve it. Amen.

DAY 114

The Victory

1 Samuel 17:51-18:4

The shepherd boy David ran right up to the fallen giant. David picked up Goliath's enormous sword. Then the soldiers watched David finish off Goliath. The enemy army started to run away as fast as they could! When he heard the news, Saul could hardly believe it. The shepherd boy had killed the giant to win the war. From that day on, David would get to live with the king, and he became best friends with the king's son Jonathan.

Dear God, When I am afraid, give me courage and strength to still do what's right. Amen.

God's Rescue

A Song by David. Psalm 9

I will praise You, oh Lord, with all of my heart. I will rejoice and be glad. I will sing to God. My enemies run away. They fall and are no more. Because God sees all and says what's right or wrong. God will be our rest and safety in our times of trouble. The bad will fall in holes they dug themselves. Those who are in need will not always be forgotten. Arise, oh God! Show the world how great You are.

Dear God, You always win the victory against Your enemies. Amen.

A Jealous King

1 Samuel 18:6-9

David was now a hero to his people. As he came home, joyful crowds ran out to greet him. "Saul has killed his thousands—" the women sang, "but now David has killed ten times more." The song made King Saul angry. Did the people like David more than him . . . their own king? Saul sat in his palace feeling jealous and full of worry. David played on his harp to try and calm Saul down.

Dear God, Help me not to get jealous of others and to show kindness to others when they are jealous of me. Amen.

The Spear

1 Samuel 18:10-15

David tried to make Saul feel better with music. But now, Saul was filled with anger instead of peace. The spear in Saul's hand went flying right at David! David rolled away though, and the spear just hit the wall. King Saul realized that God was protecting David. Now this made the king feel afraid of David as well. So King Saul sent David away to lead the army at war. David went along bravely to do a good job in all he did.

Being Brave

A Song by David. Psalm 11

In God I trust. Why should I flee like a bird though bad men want to hurt me? God is on His throne. God judges right from wrong. God knows all that is good and hates what is wrong.

DAY 119

Princess Michal

1 Samuel 18:16-19:14

Wherever David went, the people loved him. Saul's daughter, the princess, soon loved David, too. This made King Saul hate David more than ever. He decided he would finish David, once and for all. The next morning, the king's men came to get David. Princess Michal told them, "David is sick in bed." But secretly, the princess had helped David to escape. She had let David down through a window, and he had run away.

Dear God, Give me courage to help others in need. Amen.

Waiting on God

A Song by David. Psalm 27

The Lord is my light. Whom shall I fear? The Lord is my strength. Who can make me afraid? Whoever tries to hurt me will stumble and fall. So even in the middle of war, my heart won't fear. In the time of trouble, God will take me to a safe place. So for now I lift my head up singing praise. Be brave, and God will come to make your heart strong. Wait, I tell you; wait on the Lord.

Dear God, You are my strength, and I will sing praises to You. Amen.

David in Hiding

1 Samuel 20:1-24

Prince Jonathan went to find out why David ran away. David told him, "Your father, Saul, wants to kill me!" Jonathan said, "I will come back and tell you if it's true." Then Jonathan said goodbye to his best friend David and went home.

Dear God, Thank You for good friends.
Help me to be a good friend, too. Amen.

DAY 122

The Arrow

1 Samuel 20:35-42

It was time for Jonathan to tell what he had found out. He went back to the field where David was hiding. Then the prince told the news using their secret code. Jonathan shot an arrow into the air with his bow. David knew exactly what Jonathan's message meant. It was true after all. King Saul wanted to kill David. The two best friends ran to hug each other and cried. Then David said goodbye to Prince Jonathan and left.

Dear God, Whenever I have to leave my friend, give me hope that we will see each other again. Amen.

Thirst for God

A Song by David. Psalm 42

Like a deer is thirsty for water, oh God, my soul is thirsty for You. I call on You because my heart is sad. I call because it feels like waves are pushing me down. Still, I will remember Your miracles, God. I will remember Your love, day and night. When I am sad, my hope is in You. I will love You forever for You are my God.

Dear God, When I am sad, I will sing to You and feel better. Amen.

DAY 124

Bread and Sword

1 Samuel 21:1-10

David had lost his home, his job, and those he loved. He was now in danger and without food and protection. David wandered alone into a small town. There, he asked a priest if he could have some bread. Then suddenly, David saw one of Saul's men there, too. *Oh no!* thought David, *I'd better get away from here before anyone tells Saul where I am.* David asked the priest for bread and a weapon. The priest said, "I have nothing but the sword of Goliath." "That's perfect!" David said. He took the sword and ran.

Dear God, You give me what I need. You love to give good things to Your children. Amen.

DAY 125

Saul Chases David

1 Samuel 22:9-23

King Saul called for the priest of Nob and said to him, "Why did you give David bread and a sword?" The priest said, "Because David is good to the king." Saul was still angry that the priest helped David get away. "Kill him!" Saul said. David was told the news in the cave where he was hiding. "The priest died because of me," David said sadly. But more and more soldiers now came to help David against King Saul. A king who hurt servants of God was bad indeed!

Dear God, When I am sad or hear bad news, please send a friend my way to comfort me. Amen.

The Cave

1 Samuel 24:1-7

Saul and his army chased David into the wilderness. One day, the king went into a cave alone . . . the very cave where David and his friends were hiding! No one made a sound as they stayed in the shadows. King Saul did not see David sneaking toward him. So, David cut off just the smallest piece of Saul's robe. Then Saul and his soldiers left the cave without a clue. David told his friends, "Don't hurt him. Just let him go."

Saul Is Sorry

1 Samuel 24:8-17

Saul and his men were walking from the cave when they heard someone yell out, "My king!" It was David bowing on the ground outside the cave. In his hand was a cut piece of Saul's robe. "Believe that I don't want to hurt you," David said. "If I wanted to, I could have; but I only cut your robe." Saul could see that it was true and started to weep. "I was bad to you," Saul said, "but you stayed kind to me."

Dear God, Help me not to be mean to people who are mean to me but to show them Your love. Amen.

DAY 128

Staying Strong

A Song by David. Psalm 52

Why brag of naughty deeds, oh you mighty man? God's goodness is the thing that lasts forever. But you love doing evil more than doing good. You like lies more than you like hearing truth. God will pull you out just like a weed. Everyone will know you disobeyed. But God will make me strong forever just like a tree because I stay near Him. Forever I will put my trust in Him. I will praise you, O God, for all you have done, and I will hope in your good name.

Dear God, Help me to follow You even when my friends don't. Amen.

Wise Abigail

1 Samuel 25:4-35

David's friends went to a farm they knew nearby. The grumpy farmer wouldn't give them food. Now David was on his way to punish the farmer. But there on the road came Abigail bringing fine foods. "Forgive my rude husband, Lord David," said Abigail. "One day you'll be king, and then he won't matter." David said, "What wise words . . . bless God for sending you!" David took her gift of food and said, "Go in peace."

Dear God, Help me to be wise and know how to encourage others. Amen.

DAY 130

The Spear

1 Samuel 26:4-21

David sent out spies. They found out that King Saul was still chasing him. That night, David snuck up to Saul's camp in the wilderness. The king lay fast asleep with his spear next to him. David's friend begged, "Let me kill him with his spear!" Instead, David took Saul's spear and water jug. Then David climbed up a hill with them and yelled, "Why are you still chasing a tiny flea, Great King?" King Saul woke up and answered, "You didn't kill me tonight even though you could have. So I will no longer try to harm you."

Dear God, When someone hurts my feelings,
help me not to be mean back. Amen.

DAY 131

The Exile

1 Samuel 27:1-7

Saul took his men and left the desert wilderness to go home. But David had enough. Saul could not be trusted. There was only one place David would be safe from Saul: the land of Israel's enemy the Philistines! David did not know what was going to happen when he arrived in the enemy's land. But just as God had promised, David stayed safe. He made friends with a powerful enemy ruler, and everything David needed was given to him. Now David was finally safe and could rest.

Dear God, You kept David safe even with his enemies. You always keep Your promises. Amen.

Help in Trouble

A Song by David. Psalm 59

Rescue me, my God, from those who want me hurt. Save me from those who come to harm me. They lay in wait. They say bad things about me. But You will laugh at them, oh Lord, every one. So let those who do evil go make noises just like dogs that wander without finding what they seek. But I will sing, oh God, of Your power in the morning. For You helped me when I was in trouble.

Dear God, I will not be afraid because You are in charge of all people and help me in my troubles. Amen.

DAY 133

Saul Talks to a Ghost

1 Samuel 28:5-25

King Saul knew that God was not happy with him. Yet Saul needed help because the Philistines were coming. Though Samuel was already dead, Saul wanted his advice so badly. He went to see a woman who could talk with the dead. He hoped that the woman could ask the ghost of Samuel what to do. But what Samuel said was not good. It was too late for Saul. Tomorrow, God was going to let the Philistines beat him. Saul fell over on the floor, weak and afraid. The woman fed him for strength. Then Saul went home.

Dear God, When I need help, I will come ask You and trust that You will help me. Amen.

David Mourns

2 Samuel 1:1-27

A soldier could hardly wait to tell David the news: King Saul and Prince Jonathan both died in battle. "I took Saul's crown and bracelet, My Lord," said the soldier. "And I brought them here for you." But David was not glad. He had loved the two men. David cried, "Saul and Jonathan were loved by many. They were faster than eagles, stronger than lions. Now cry Israel; your mighty king and his son are no more."

Dear God, All of us are sinners and need You to help us. I want to be Your helper to any person, good or bad. Amen.

DAY 135

A King, Good and True

2 Samuel 3:1-5:5

A son of Saul now wore the crown. Yet some felt David should be the king instead. The people began to fight. They fought and they fought until at last, they could agree. A king must be brave, and a king must be kind. But most of all, a king must obey God. The crown was put on David's head. Israel now had a king, good and true.

Dear God, Everything You say happens,
and what You promise comes true. Amen.

DAY 136

Sing with Joy

A Song by David. Psalm 66

Make a joyful shout, all the earth! Say to God, "How great are Your works! All the world worships You. All the world sings praises to You." God made a path right through the sea. The people could walk across it. Hard times came, but God brought us through them. He led the way into joy.

Dear God, Everything I have comes from You. Thank You for leading me through good and bad times. Amen.

The Rule of David

2 Samuel 5:6-25

King David asked God for help in all he did, in where to go, and in how to rule. A king that would obey was a king that made God happy. David's family grew bigger. David's army grew stronger. The people could trust King David to do what was right, to do what was fair. Never was a land more mighty than David's. Never was a king more loved.

Dear God, I want to know you more and more as I grow up so I can be like you. Amen.

DAY 138

The Lost Ark

2 Samuel 6:1-22

The city was filled with shouts of joy. It was David and his army bringing home the ark! The king wore only a cloth. He was dancing for God with all his might. Princess Michal saw the parade and gave a frown. "How embarrassing to see the king dance like that!" she said. David said, "To you I might be an embarrassment, but I am dancing for God who made me king."

Dear God, I will not worry what others think when I praise You. Help me to worship You everywhere. Amen.

DAY 139

The Crippled Son

2 Samuel 9:1-13

The boy felt afraid. His grandfather, King Saul, had tried to kill David! So what would David do now that he was king? It was hard to run away with crippled legs. But King David remembered how much he loved Saul's son Jonathan. And here was Jonathan's only son. "I give you," said David, "all the land of Saul and a place to always eat at my table." The crippled son of Jonathan was now like the king's own son.

Dear God, All that I have is from You, so help me to be generous and share what I have with others. Amen.

Bathsheba

2 Samuel 11:1-27

King David didn't go with his army to war like he was supposed to. One day looking down from his roof, he saw a woman named Bathsheba and fell in love with her. Bathsheba already had a husband, but David did not care. He got rid of her husband so he could have her for himself even though it was wrong.

DAY 141

Nathan's Story

2 Samuel 12:1-13

The prophet Nathan had a message. He told King David of a rich man who stole a tiny lamb. Though the rich man had many lambs of his own, he stole the lamb from someone who had only one little lamb. "What an awful thing to do!" David cried. "But David," said Nathan, "you did the same thing. You stole a soldier's wife, and then you had him killed." Nathan told David that God would punish him. With a sad heart, King David bowed his head. He would go and tell God how sorry he was for what he had done.

Dear God, When You show me what I have done wrong, it is always because You love me. Amen.

DAY 142

David Is Sorry

A Song by David. Psalm 69

Save me, oh God! I am sinking in muck. I cry so much I can hardly see. You know each one of my foolish ways. Nothing is hidden from You. Don't let my friends be ashamed. See how I cried and dressed in rags. Pull me from the muck, oh God. Hear me, for I know Your love is good.

Dear God, Even though I can't see you, teach my heart to know Your truth. Amen.

The Lost Son

2 Samuel 12:14-25

David and Bathsheba had a baby. But like Nathan had said, God punished David and took the baby back. David cried so much that the servants were worried he would cry forever. When the boy died, David got up. He changed his clothes. Then, he went to spend time with God. The servants asked how David could feel better so fast. "Tears will not bring back my son," David answered. God would bless David again at just the right time. Soon, David had another son named Solomon, and God smiled down.

Dear God, I will have hard times. Help me to feel better after bad things happen. Amen.

The Dream of a Temple

1 Chronicles 22

King David had a dream of a resting place for God where all could go and pray and where the ark could be kept forever. "A house for God," said David, "must be magnificent! Grander than grand. Famous, near and far." It must be made with the richest trees and with nails of iron, with the strongest stones and the very finest cloth, sparkling in and out with silver and gold. Yes—when peace comes to the land at last, then God would get the house that God deserves, and Solomon would build it.

Dear God, Help me to dream big dreams that will help others come to know you. Amen.

DAY 145

David Runs Away

2 Samuel 15

David's other son Prince Absalom had good looks. He had charm, as well. The prince was even nice to his servants. Was there any in all the land who did not like Absalom? Before long, he got to thinking. *Why should I stay a prince when I could be king?* His father soon heard about the plan. King David had never been so sad. How could David fight his own son? David would hide awhile instead. No matter how awful Absalom acted, his father did not want him hurt.

Dear God, Even when it's hard, help me to do the right thing. Amen.

God Is Good

A Song by David. 2 Samuel 22:1-21

God is my rock of strength, my tower of safety. When the waves had swept me up and the floods made me afraid, I called on God, and He heard me up in heaven. Then the earth shook. God was coming to my rescue. He pulled me from the waves and brought me to a safe place. God rewarded me because I had done right.

Dear God, You rescue me and keep me safe. I will not be afraid. Amen.

DAY 147

Song of Sorrow

A Prayer of David. Psalm 86

Bow down Your ear, oh God, and hear me. I am poor and needy. Save Your servant who trusts in You! I cry to You all day long. Oh God, the proud have stood to fight me. They do not look to God. But You, oh Lord, are full of goodness. Come and give me strength.

Dear God, Even though I can't see You,
teach my heart to know Your truth. Amen.

The Last Song

A Song of David. Psalm 108

God, I am still the same. My heart has never changed. So I will sing and praise You even though I am now a famous king. I will wake the morning because Your love is as high as the clouds. Who else has always helped me but you, God?

Dear God, No matter what I do or where I go, I will still praise You. I will thank you when I wake up each morning. Amen.

A New King

1 Kings 1:15-34

David was sick, and he was now too old to rule. It was time to have a new king. The prophet Nathan and Bathsheba stood next to David's bed. They listened as he told them what to do. "Take Solomon," said David, "and put him on my mule. Blow a horn, and yell 'God save King Solomon!' And he will then be your new king."

Dear God, Sometimes there are sad times. Help me to know you are there to love me through them. Amen.

DAY 150

A Father's Blessing

1 Kings 2:1-10

David was not well. He called for Solomon. "I'm meeting my end just like any life must," said David. "So be strong, and follow God. Take care of the people by ruling wisely." Then the great king of Israel passed on.

Dear God, Help me to honor my parents
and listen to what they say. Amen.

DAY 151

Words of a King

2 Samuel 23:3-4

King David said these words of God before he died: God says one who rules must be fair. He should keep his faith in God. Then he will be like the sun in the morning, shining after the rain and making grass grow.

Dear God, I want to be a blessing by being fair and by being faithful to You. Amen.

Solomon's Wish

1 Kings 3:3-9

The new king gave thanks to God. That very night, God visited him in a dream. "Make a wish," said God to Solomon. What was it that the king wanted most? "Oh God," said Solomon, "I am still just a kid. Help me to rule and to know what is fair. Make me wise—so that I know what's right and what's wrong."

DAY 153

The Promise

1 Kings 3:10-15

God was glad. King Solomon did not ask to be rich. He did not ask to be famous. What Solomon wanted was to be wise. "I will grant your wish," God told him. "You shall have a wise heart like no one else." God would even give Solomon a bonus. "Since your wish was good," said God, "I will make you rich and famous as well." Solomon woke up from the dream. He praised God for what he had told him. Then Solomon hurried home to give his servants a feast!

Dear God, Help me not to be greedy but to be happy with what I get. Amen.

Who Is Wise?

Wise Words of Solomon. Proverbs 1

In order to be wise, you must first put your trust in God. Next, listen to your father. Obey your mother's rules. God will give you wisdom if you look for it like treasure. A wise heart is your light to keep you safe and happy.

Dear God, Make me wise like Solomon, and help me do what is right. Amen.

Solomon, the Judge

1 Kings 3-4

The whole land had a broken heart the day King David died. Could they ever love a new king after David? Yet like his father, Solomon was strong and wise. The people soon could see that their new king loved God very much. But there was also something more. Solomon loved to learn. He thought about ideas from far and wide. And Solomon was wise. He knew how to decide what was fair. Solomon was not only a king—he was a judge as well. The people could trust King Solomon to learn what was true and to do what was right.

Dear God, Teach me to be wise like Solomon. I
always want to do what is true and right. Amen.

DAY 156

David's Dream

1 Kings 5:2-5

David had been king in a time of war. Now his son was in charge. Wise Solomon made friends with Egypt and with other lands far away. At last, there was peace. King Solomon knew what it was time to do. "My father did not get to build what he dreamed of building," said Solomon to the people. "So now we are going to build it . . . a house for God." The people could hardly wait to begin. At last they would have a temple for worshiping God!

Dear God, You gave Solomon a big job to do.
I want to do big things for You too. Amen.

DAY 157

A House for God

1 Kings 5-6:37

The best of the best had been called to help. They were making a house like no one had seen. Huge stones were cut to lay the floor. Pillars were molded to hold the roof. The artists cut wood into angels and flowers. Then, all was covered with gold. There was gold across the floor and the altar and the walls. The whole place sparkled and gleamed.

Dear God, Whatever I do with my hands,
I want it to be a gift to You. Amen.

The House that Solomon Built

1 Kings 7:51-8

The house for God was done. Time to put in the treasures that David had collected. The priests very carefully took up the ark. The shining glory of God filled up the building as though God were right there beside them filling every heart with peace and joy. "God," said Solomon. "I built this house for You. Even though Your real home is in heaven. But now I pray," the king went on, "that You will watch over all those who come here, listen as they pray, and forgive them."

Dear God, Thank You for church where we can go and worship You and learn about the Bible with friends. Amen.

DAY 159

Run Like Deer

Wise Words of Solomon. Proverbs 6:1-5

Listen to me, child, and keep yourself from trouble. When you have done a wrong thing, do not go try to hide. Instead, work hard to fix it, not later but right away. That way you are freed like a deer who runs away from a hunter.

Watch an Ant

Wise Words of Solomon. Proverbs 6:6-11

Go and watch an ant. Learn all about it to be made wise. Watch how no one tells an ant what it should do. Yet still the ant collects its food the whole summer long. In fall the ant is hard at work as well.

Dear God, Just like the ant You made, I will do my work without being asked. Amen.

DAY 161

Queen of Sheba

1 Kings 10:1-7

A king, so great and so wise? The Queen of Sheba had to see for herself. She headed off in a grand parade of camels and servants. The queen brought Solomon the riches of her land . . . gold and silver, jewels and spices. Now what did the queen want in return? She would ask the wise King Solomon the questions of her heart. They talked and talked. At last, the queen said, "So it is true! You are even more wise than I had heard."

Dear God, You made different kinds of people from
many countries. I will be kind to them all. Amen.

DAY 162

The Richest King

1 Kings 10:9-29

"Bless God!" the Queen of Sheba declared. "He must love Israel to give them such a wise king." Solomon thanked her and added the gifts she brought him to his piles of treasure. The Queen of Sheba was not his only visitor. People came from everywhere to ask the king's advice. Each gave him gifts of treasure or animals. Wise Solomon was the richest king on earth.

Dear God, Solomon honored You and was a wise King for You. Help me to honor You in all I do. Amen.

Be Glad

Wise Words of Solomon. Proverbs 17:1,22

Better to have gladness with just a crust of bread than to have a house with lots of food that is full of sadness. A glad heart is a healthy heart. Joy is like a vitamin, but sadness in your heart just tires you out.

Dear God, Help me to be happy with what I have and not be upset and whiney all the time. Amen.

God Knows You

Wise Words of Solomon. Proverbs 20

God made all, and God knows all. If someone is a good person, he will do good things. God sees if you are doing right and if you are being fair. So don't do wrong when others do. Ask God to make things right. God's light shines in your heart, so you can see the good things and get rid of the bad.

Dear God, You know what I feel and what I think.
Make my heart and mind good and pure. Amen.

DAY 165

The King's True Love

Song of Songs: 1-2

I love you very much and I want everyone to know. You are my special one and you make me so happy. You are beautiful like a flower. You are strong like a young stag. We belong together you and I.

Dear God, Thank You for all the people who love me and for showing me how to love others. Amen.

Solomon in Love

Song of Songs: 3

One night I couldn't find you. I went out and was looking for you everywhere. I asked for you because I missed you. Finally I found you. I gave you the biggest hug, and I didn't let go before we got back home safely.

Dear God, Thank You that no matter what happens You will never let go of me. Amen.

DAY 167

A Good Woman

Wise Words of Solomon. Proverbs 31:10-31

A good woman is worth far more than rubies. She is wise and hard-working. She gives to the poor and helps the needy. She makes sure her family has everything they need. She loves God and is loved by her family.

Dear God, Help me to serve others and make wise choices and follow You. Amen.

God Is Fair

Ecclesiastes 12:9-14

Above all other things, know that God is true. Keeping His commandments is the most important deed. For everything we do, God will surely see. God also knows each secret, kind or sneaky.

Dear God, You are true. Help me to be truthful and trustworthy and to obey your commandments. Amen.

DAY 169

The Greatest King

1 Kings 11:1-13

King Solomon got more and more rich. He got more and more famous. There was no king so mighty and wise. Solomon had made the most wonderful temple for God, but he stopped loving God with all his heart. He started serving other gods, which was against God's law. So God brought war again, but God's promise stayed true. Solomon was remembered as the wisest king who ever lived.

Dear God, Keep my heart from wanting to go away
from You. Help me to always love You. Amen

A Time for All

Ecclesiastes 3:1-14

There is a time to plant. There is a time to pick. There is a time to laugh and a time to cry. There is a time to win and to lose. A time for war and for peace. God planned all things perfect in His time.

Dear God, I will not worry because there is a time for everything, and You are always in control. Amen.

Son of Solomon

1 Kings 11:41-12:20

Solomon's son was now the King. He called for the wise men to give him some advice. "The people want to know if I will work them as hard as my father did. What should I tell them?" asked the new king. The wise men said, "Be kind, and they will help you." The king wanted to hear what his friends thought, as well. The young men said to the new king, "Tell the people that you will make them work harder than your father ever did." The king did not listen to the wise men but to his friends. *This new king was not wise at all,* thought the people.

Dear God, Help me to listen to my parents and grandparents who have lived a long time and are smart. Amen.

The Prophet Elijah

1 Kings 16:29-17:3

God loved his prophet Elijah, and Elijah loved God. Elijah knew when God was happy with people. He also knew when God was upset. And Elijah had a message from God for the king. The king had been praying to other gods . . . and there was little else that made God more angry than that! "Now there will not be rain," Elijah told the King. Then Elijah ran from the city to hide in nature.

A Prophet's Work

Words of a Prophet. Isaiah 61:1-3

The Spirit of God is with me because He has given me things to go tell to the meek. He has sent me to heal the heart that is broken and set free all those who are prisoners. God has sent me to tell when He's angry and to comfort all those who have lost. To give beauty for ashes and trade pain in for joy. To give joy to hearts that are sad.

Dear God, Just like You spoke to people through the prophets, give me courage to speak Your truth. Amen.

DAY 174

Elijah and the Ravens

1 Kings 17:2-6

Elijah was hiding out by a stream. He had water to drink, and God kept him safe. Suddenly, Elijah saw shadows on the ground. It was big, black birds—swooping right at him! What was it the birds dropped from their beaks? It was chunks of bread and meat. God had sent ravens to bring food for Elijah to eat. The birds brought food each day in the morning and night.

Dear God, You sent birds with food to provide for Elijah.
I know You will always provide for me too. Amen.

The Woman with Sticks

1 Kings 17:7-13

The stream where Elijah was dried up. God had a new plan. He sent Elijah into town. A poor woman was picking up sticks. Elijah asked her for some water and a little bread. The woman had no bread only a bit of flour and oil. "Do not worry," Elijah told her. "Make some bread to share with me, and God will make sure you will not run out of flour or oil."

Dear God, Help me to listen to Your directions and follow them. Amen.

Her Last Meal

1 Kings 17:14-16

The woman did just what Elijah said. She went home to make him bread. She got out the jars of flour and oil and began to pour out what was left inside. But then—could this be true? She could pour and pour, but the jars stayed full! The woman shared her bread with gladness. And like Elijah had said, she did not run out.

Dear God, I want to be like Elijah and listen for Your directions so I can obey them and see great miracles! Amen.

The Sick Son

1 Kings 17:17-24

The woman had a son who got very sick. "Bring him to me," said Elijah. He laid the boy down on his own bed. "Oh God," prayed Elijah, "help this child!" God heard Elijah and made the boy well. His mother gave Elijah a big, happy smile. "Now I know the truth," she said. "God is with you. And all you say is true."

Dear God, You have power over death.
Nothing will make me afraid. Amen.

Fire on the Mountain

1 Kings 18:1-39

Prophet Elijah told the king to meet him on a mountain. They were going to see who the real God was. The king went first. The king's prophets called to their god Baal. They called and called . . . but no one answered. All was still. Now it was Elijah's turn. "Oh, God," cried Elijah, "please show that You are real." Suddenly—*boom!* The pile of sticks at the alter burst into fire! The one God who is real and true had answered.

Dear God, You are the one, real
God. I will believe in You. Amen.

DAY 179

The Watchman

Words of a Prophet. Ezekiel 33:1-9

God told me that if a person has the job of keeping watch, they have to warn others when they see danger coming. Then if any hear the warning but act like they don't care, it is their own fault if they get hurt. But if the watcher sees a danger and does not try to warn, then any person hurt will be the watchman's fault. God said, "You as prophet are the watcher for the people I love. So hear the things I say, and if there is danger, go and warn my people."

An Angel at the Tree

1 Kings 19:1-6

Elijah had proven who the real God is, and the king was not too happy about it. "Don't worry," said the queen. She was going to punish Elijah. So Elijah ran away as fast as he could. Elijah stopped to rest under a tree, and he felt ready to give up. He had finally fallen asleep when he felt a touch. "Wake up," said an angel. "It's time to eat." Elijah opened his eyes . . . to freshly baked bread made just for him!

Dear God, Thank You for helping me not give up but to keep following You. Amen.

The Quiet Voice

1 Kings 19:11-13

Elijah went to meet God on top of a hill. A strong wind blew. *Smash!* went the rocks. But God was not in the strong wind. Next, the ground shook. It was an earthquake! God was not in the earthquake either. Then came a fire. But God was not in the fire. At last, Elijah heard only a quiet whisper. And in the whisper, there was God.

Dear God, You are so powerful, but You come to us with softness and kindness. Amen.

Farmer Elisha

1 Kings 19:16-21

God was going to give Elijah some help. A farmer named Elisha would be his assistant. So Elijah went to call Elisha from his field. Elisha could not *wait* to start his new job! "May I just kiss my parents goodbye?" said Elisha. "Then I will come with you." Elisha went home and made a big feast. Then Elisha left his farm to help Elijah.

Dear God, If You call me, I will follow You gladly. Amen.

DAY 183

Garden for a King

1 Kings 21:1-15

King Ahab was more grumpy than ever. He lay on his bed all day and would not eat. "Why so sad?" the queen asked him. The king wanted a garden he could not buy. The queen said, "Don't worry. I will get it for you." Then she told lies so that the garden's owner got in trouble and was killed. "There, there," the queen said to the king. "Go and be happy in your new garden."

Dear God, It is not good to be jealous of what others have or try and get it from them. Amen.

DAY 184

The Sorry King

1 Kings 21:16-29

The king was on his way to his new garden. Little did he know . . . Elijah was on his way, too. God had told Elijah the bad thing the queen had done. And God sent Elijah to tell the king He was angry. The king knew that Elijah was telling the truth. He fell on the ground full of sadness. He was sorry about the trick to get the garden. Since the king was sorry, God was kind.

Dear God, Help me to be happy with what I have and not want something else. Amen.

The King's Question

1 Kings 22:4-17

"Should we go to war?" the king wanted to know. "Why don't you ask God," said his friend. So the king called all the wise men to ask them. Each of the wise men said he should go to war, yet there was one more wise man to ask, the prophet Micah. The king said, "Tell me that you agree with them." Micah told the king, "I will only tell you what is true. And God says you had better *not* go to war, oh King."

Dear God, I will do what You tell me to do and not what others say is right. Amen.

DAY 186

The True Prophet

1 Kings 22:26-37

Prophet Micah had made the king very angry. How could a prophet tell a king not to go to war? The king threw Micah in jail. Then he went to war. But . . . just like Micah had warned, the king lost and was killed in battle.

Dear God, Help me to not be selfish and try to
get my way but to do what is best. Amen.

DAY 187

A Prophet Speaks

Words of a Prophet. Obadiah 1

Land of Edom, you will pay for being mean to my people. You were too proud of yourselves to see you did wrong. You made high nests like you were eagles. "Who can bring us down?" Edom said. God will bring you down; that's who. You should not have stood by while others hurt. You should not have taken what was not yours. The bad you did to others will now come to you.

Dear God, You will give a punishment to those who are mean to others. I don't have to be mean back. Amen.

The Fallen King

2 Kings 1:1-8

King Ahaziah, the son of King Ahab, had a bad fall, and now he was sick in bed. He told his servants, "Go ask my gold statue if I will heal." But on their way . . . here came the prophet Elijah. And Elijah did not look happy at all. The king should have talked to God not to a statue. Elijah told the servants that the king would stay sick. They went to tell the king. "Who said this?" he growled. "A man wearing prophet clothes of animal hair and leather," the servants said. The king knew it was Elijah.

Dear God, You are the one who makes people better. I will trust You to do it. Amen.

Fire of Elijah

2 Kings 1:9-15

Elijah saw the soldiers coming to the hill. The king had sent his army to come and get him. But Elijah was not afraid of swords. He had God. And Elijah could make fire come down from Heaven with only words. *Poof,* and the army went up in smoke. So the king sent more soldiers. And more. But now, the soldiers were the ones afraid! "Ok," said Elijah, "I will come with you and tell the king what the Lord says."

Dear God, I will tell Your truth even
if it makes others mad. Amen.

Love of Elisha

2 Kings 2:1-6

Elisha loved his master with all his heart. When Elijah said, "Rest here while I go to Bethel," Elisha answered, "I want to come along and help." So together, they went to Bethel. Elijah said, "Rest a bit while I go work in Jericho." "No thanks, I will come and help you," said Elisha. Elijah said, "Take a break while I go to the Jordan River." Elisha said, "No, I will never leave your side."

Dear God, I want to be a good helper even when I am tired or need to rest. Amen.

Elijah's Goodbye

2 Kings 2:1-11

Elisha had stayed with Elijah in good times and bad. And Elisha knew it was almost time for his master to go. They were walking along one day when a ride came from heaven. It was horses pulling a chariot ablaze with fire! Then a big gust of wind whirled around them. The wind picked Elijah up, and he was gone. Elijah had been taken to heaven to be with God.

Dear God, You prepared Elisha to take over the job of Elijah. You will prepare me for your works as well. Amen.

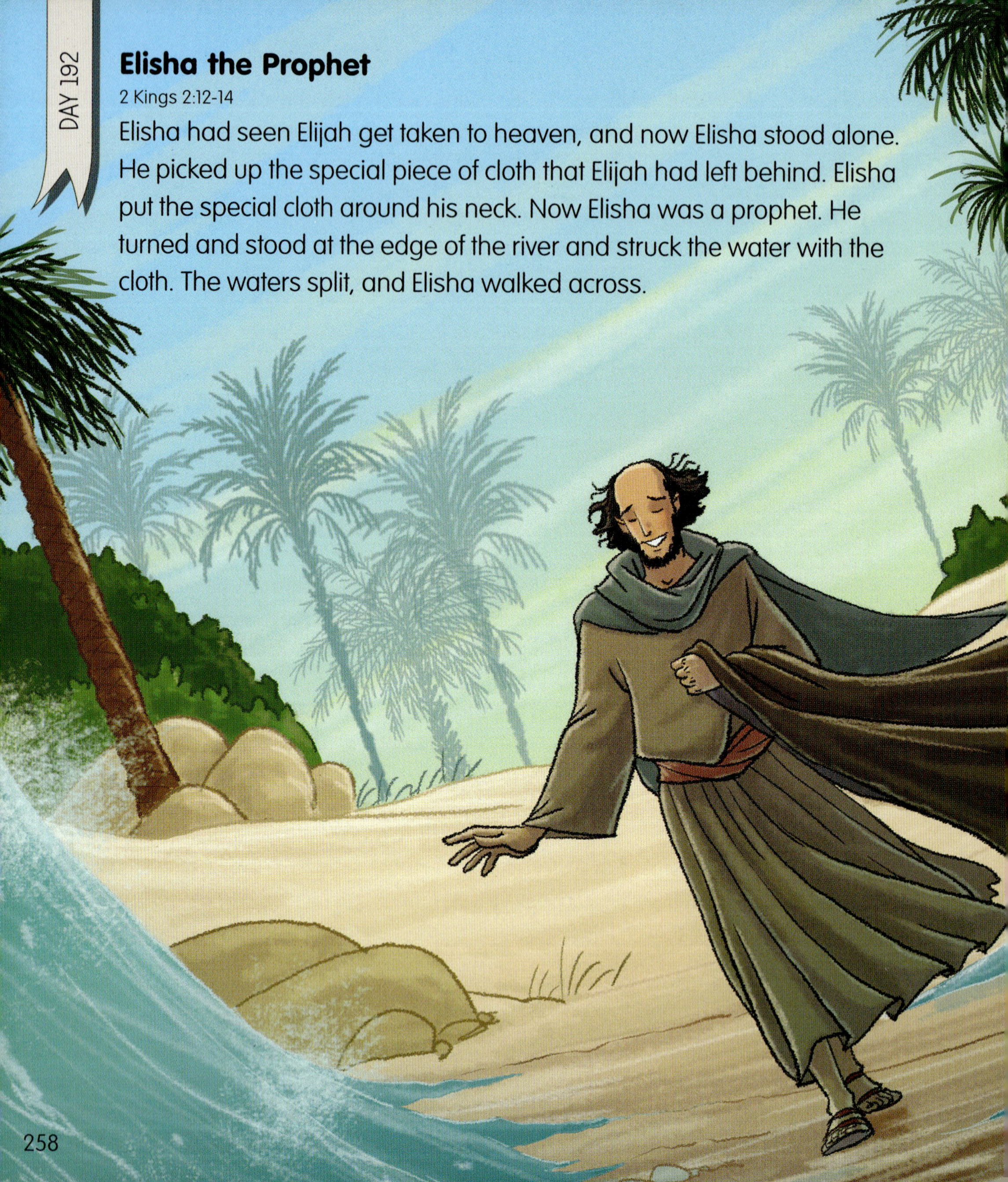

DAY 192

Elisha the Prophet

2 Kings 2:12-14

Elisha had seen Elijah get taken to heaven, and now Elisha stood alone. He picked up the special piece of cloth that Elijah had left behind. Elisha put the special cloth around his neck. Now Elisha was a prophet. He turned and stood at the edge of the river and struck the water with the cloth. The waters split, and Elisha walked across.

Dear God, When You give me a big job to do, I will not be afraid but do it with all my heart. Amen.

DAY 193

Elisha Answers

2 Kings 2:15-18

Elisha went to Jericho. The company of prophets came out to met him. They could see Elisha now had Elijah's power. So they bowed down in front of Elisha. Elisha told them that Elijah was taken to heaven. "Let's go look for him anyway," they said, "just to make sure he is not stuck somewhere." But Elijah was no where. Elisha was now in charge.

Dear God, You put the right people in charge, and I will respect my leaders. Amen.

The Poisoned Spring

2 Kings 2:19-22

The people of Jericho went to see Prophet Elisha. "Look," they said. "The water in our spring is bad." Elisha told them to bring a pot of salt. Then he threw the salt into the poisoned spring. Elisha said that God would now heal the spring. There would be no more death because of bad water. That very day the water was made clean. God had fixed the spring just like Elisha said.

Dear God, You do great miracles all the time. You are in control. Amen.

Three Kings

2 Kings 3:10-27

Three kings went to Elisha for help. They all came to tell Elisha that their armies were about to lose to the enemy. "Not true," said Elisha. "God says you will win." So the kings went with gladness to meet their victory.

Dear God, Even kings get scared and come to You. I will come to You for courage. Amen.

A Pot of Oil

2 Kings 4:1-7

A woman could not pay what she owed. So now, they were going to put her children to work. Could the prophet Elisha help? Elisha told her what to do, and she obeyed every word. First, she filled a room in her house with empty pots. Then the woman started to pour the oil that she had left. Soon, every pot was full . . . the oil had not run out! Happy again, she went to sell the oil and paid the money she owed.

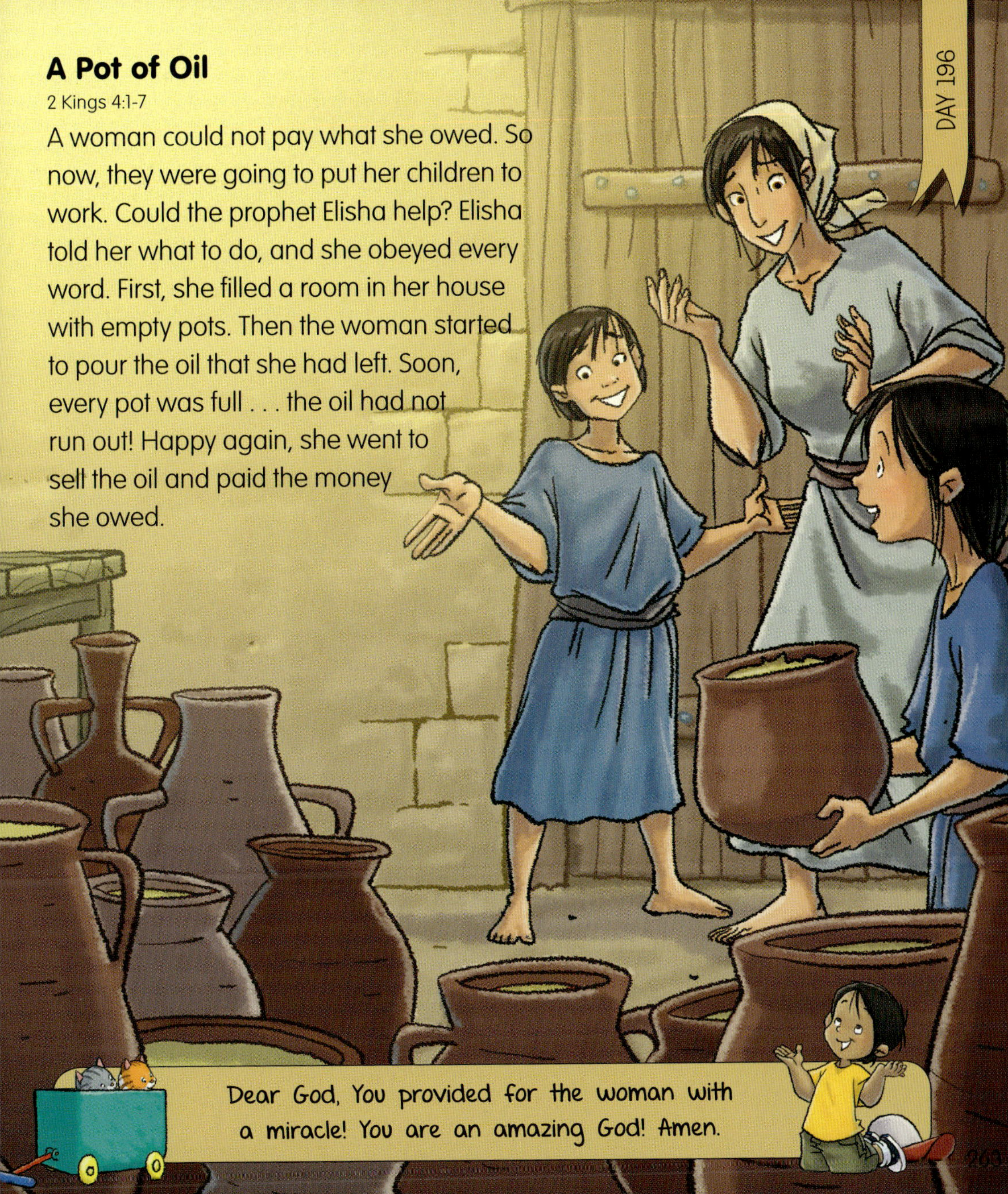

Dear God, You provided for the woman with a miracle! You are an amazing God! Amen.

DAY 197

A Great Woman

2 Kings 4:8-16

There lived a woman in another land who was kind and rich. She knew in her heart that Elisha was a prophet of God. When he passed, she stopped him to give him bread. In her home, she made him a bed to sleep on. Elisha said, "What can I do to pay you back?" But the woman would not tell him a wish. A servant told Elisha that the woman had no children. Elisha called her in and said, "Soon, you will have a son."

Dear God, I will serve others who are workers
for You and help them do their jobs. Amen.

DAY 198

The Promised Son

2 Kings 4:16-26

Like Elisha had promised, the woman had a son. One day, her son went to find his father in the field. "My head," said the son, "my head." He was very sick, so sick that he died the same day. But his mother believed in God and had faith. "It will be alright," she told her husband. Then she rode as fast as she could to get Elisha. God gave her this son one time; He could do it again.

Dear God, When someone is sick, I don't need to fear because You are in control. Amen.

DAY 199

The Boy Awakes

2 Kings 4:24-35

The woman who believed told no one her son died. She galloped on her donkey to get Elisha. Elisha saw her coming . . . and looking very upset. So Elisha went with her to look at the boy. Elisha prayed. He put his hands on the child's hands. He walked back and forth. Was it going to work? At last the boy's hands started to get warm. He sneezed seven times, and then he opened his eyes.

Dear God, You are so mighty that You can make people come alive again! Amen.

God Will Call

Words of a Prophet. Micah 6:8-9

God has shown you what is good. Be fair and kind no matter what. Walk with God and listen to Him. One who is wise will hear God call.

Dear God, Thank you for showing me what is good. I will be fair and kind. Amen.

DAY 201

I Will Make You Strong

Words of a Prophet. Micah 4:6-13

"In the end," says God, "I will gather all who were pushed away. Those who were hurting, I will come and collect. I will make them a nation strong for God. So when you are taken to a foreign country as captives, I will rescue you. I will make you strong like iron, and I will give you back what your enemies took from you."

Dear God, You are coming again to save all who believe in You. Help me always be ready. Amen.

The Little Maid

2 Kings 5:1-5

A girl was captured! Now she was a slave. She was brought to a new land to work as a maid. But the girl was brave. She stayed good and true, so they let her be the maid for the captain's wife. The captain, Naaman, had a skin sickness. The girl told his wife, "I know who can make him well—Prophet Elisha." So Naaman took gifts of silver and gold and went to look for Elisha. The slave girl had given help instead of anger.

Dear God, Even when others treat me badly, I will still try to help them. Amen.

DAY 203

The Caring Servant

2 Kings 5:9-13

Elisha didn't come out but sent his servant to meet Naaman saying, "Go wash yourself in the river Jordan and your skin will be healed." But Naaman went away angry. He said, "I wanted Elisha to come himself and do something to heal me. I could have washed in a river at home!" His servant said, "Why not give it a try? Washing in a river is, after all, very easy."

Dear God, Thank You that You always
send help at the right time. Amen.

DAY 204

The Captain Healed

2 Kings 5:14-15

So Captain Naaman agreed to give it a try. He would dip himself in the Jordan river seven times. He went into the water and dipped down one, two, three times . . . still he was not healed. Four, five, six . . . then Naaman dipped in the water one last time. When he came up and looked at his skin, it was as good as new. "Now I know there is a true God in Israel," said the happy captain.

Dear God, Help me to always believe that Your way is the right way. Amen.

The Floating Axe

2 Kings 6:1-6

The sons of the prophets wanted a new home. Prophet Elisha was going to help them build it. They were cutting wood when an axe went flying. It landed in the river with a *splash*. Then it sank. The man who lost the axe looked very upset. "Master," he cried, "that axe was one I *borrowed!*" So Elisha threw a stick where the axe had sunk. Up came the heavy axe floating like a feather!

Dear God, You give us miracles to help us believe in You. But help me to follow You anyway. Amen.

God of Plenty

2 Kings 7:1-16

It was a time of war, and people were hungry. The prophet Elisha told them not to worry. God was on his way to help. Elisha promised that by tomorrow there would be plenty to eat. At the enemy camp, a mighty sound was heard . . . a huge army was coming! They left camp and ran. But the sound had come from God and not from any army. The next day everyone feasted on all the food the enemy left behind.

Dear God, You always know what I need, and You give it to me. I trust in You for everything. Amen.

Spring Always Comes

Words of a Prophet. Joel 2:21-22

Fear not, oh land, but be glad and rejoice! God is good, and He will do great things. Do not be afraid, all you creatures of the wild. In every place, the spring will come again.

Dear God, You make the seasons change and take care of the whole earth. Amen.

A King Is Made

2 Kings 9:1-13

Elisha called one of the young prophets to him. "Take this box of oil," said Prophet Elisha, "and go to Jehu's house. Pour it on his head in secret. Then say, 'God makes you king over Israel.'" Jehu's friends had seen the young prophet come and go. "What was *that* all about?" they asked. So Jehu told his friends just what had happened. They blew on trumpets and yelled, "Jehu is KING!"

Dear God, You are the one who puts people in charge. I will honor Your decision. Amen.

DAY 209

Jonah and the Whale

Jonah 1

God asked Jonah for his help to go and tell a city to stop doing bad things and to worship God. But Jonah ran away instead. He tried to sail across the sea to hide out in a land far away. God knew just where Jonah was and sent a mighty storm. The sailors were afraid, but Jonah asked them to throw him into the waters. When they did, the waters became calm. A whale then swallowed Jonah up where Jonah was safe inside.

Dear God, No matter where I go, You always know where I am and are always with me. Amen.

Jonah's Second Chance

Jonah 2-4

Inside the whale, Jonah prayed to God, "I was wrong to try and hide!" So God had the whale spit Jonah out. Then Jonah did what God asked and went to the city where the people did not know God. Jonah told them to stop doing wrong and to believe in God. The ruler and the people believed in God and were saved.

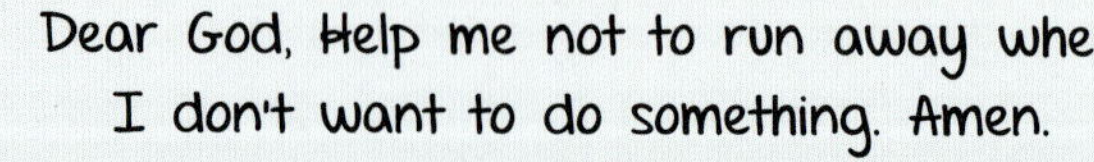

Dear God, Help me not to run away when I don't want to do something. Amen.

Land of Waste

Words of a Prophet. Joel 1-2

The land is dry and the farmer's harvest is ruined. The people are sad—for they lost everything. But if they turn back to God and say sorry, God will give them back everything. There will be plenty of food, and people will be happy again. For God is full of love, and He cares about His people.

Dear God, Help me to always love You and to always come back to You when I wander away. Amen.

The Last King

2 Kings 17:1-14

A dark cloud had come over Israel. Their king did not care what God had to say. And the people did things God had told them not to do. They made new gods and prayed to them in secret. Yet nothing is secret from God. The king was caught by the enemy and put in jail. The prophets told the people to turn from evil. But they would not listen. They no longer believed.

Dear God, You are the only real God,
and I will believe only in You. Amen.

DAY 213

God Will Forgive

Words of a Prophet. Micah 7:18-20

Is there anyone as good to you as God? Who forgives the things done wrong if we just ask? Who will not walk away—even if we make bad choices? God will not stay angry. He is happy to be kind. He will come and forgive our wrongs. God will toss sin into the deepest sea. He will give out every good thing ever promised. God will give all He promised in days of old.

Dear God, I pray You lead me in each step I take and forgive me when I make a mistake. Amen.

Israel Is Lost

2 Kings 17:6; 1 Chronicles 9:1

Since the people of Israel would not listen to God, he had to let their enemy win to get their attention. The people were taken to the city of Babylon far away. They had not obeyed God. They had not listened. So now, they would have to work in a strange new land. While they lived in a far away land, God sent them prophets to show them their bad choices and to tell them how much God loved them and wanted them to worship Him again.

Dear God, You are sad when I disobey, and You correct me so I will stop making bad choices. Amen.

God Calls a Prophet

Jeremiah 1:4-8

"I knew you before I made you," said God to the young boy Jeremiah. "I blessed you before you were born. I had my plan for you already picked out . . . to go speak for me all over the world." Then Jeremiah answered God, "But, God! I cannot speak because I am only a child." And God said, "Don't say, 'I am only a child.' Don't be afraid because I will go with you."

Dear God, Thank You for making me and having a great plan for my life. Amen.

Daniel Is Chosen

Daniel 1:1-21

The enemy king, Nebuchadnezzar, had taken more of God's people captive. The king wanted the smartest and best of the young men to work for him. Daniel and his friends obeyed God's plan, and it made them the healthiest and smartest of all. So the king picked them to serve in his palace.

Dear God, Help me to trust that your plan for my life will always be the best one. I want to obey You over any other. Amen.

DAY 217

The King's Dream

Daniel 2:1-16

The king was in a very bad mood. "Tell me," he grumbled, "what was the strange dream I had." The wise men looked at each other. They were worried. "But no one can know what you dreamed," they said. *Ha,* thought the king, *and they call themselves wise!* "Kill them," the king barked. Then came a voice that had not been called. "Wait," said Daniel. "Let me pray and ask God what your dream was and what it means."

Dear God, Help me to be a peacemaker and
bring peace to whomever I meet. Amen.

DAY 218

Daniel Answers

Daniel 2:16-48

Daniel had a very big problem to pray about. What would happen if he did not guess the king's dream? That night, God came to the rescue. God told Daniel about the king's dream as Daniel slept. Daniel went and told the king what God had said. The king was thrilled! "Your God is truly great," he said. Then the king made Daniel ruler and chief over all the wise men.

Dear God, You give wisdom and understanding to Your children when we ask. Amen.

God Is Good

Words of a Prophet. Daniel 2:20-23

Bless the name of God! You are wise, and You are strong. You know everything, and nothing is hidden from you. You control all things, God. You give power to kings and can take it away again. Thank you for answering my prayer when I asked for help. You have told me the meaning of the king's dream.

Dear God, You are strong and wise, and You know everything. Amen.

DAY 220

Three Friends

Daniel 2:48-3:12

Shadrach, Meshach, and Abednego were Daniel's friends. Now that Daniel was a ruler, his friends got good jobs as wise men, too. Some in the land felt that it was unfair and that the wise men had it so easy. But Daniel and his friends kept their eyes on God.

Dear God, I will always keep my eyes on You even when everything is good. Amen.

The Golden God

Daniel 3:1-17

The gold statue was great and tall and gleaming. "Come one, come all!" said the king, "and pray to the new god that I have made." Yet Shadrach, Meshach, and Abednego did not obey. "Throw them in the fire!" the king told his soldiers. The men who had been jealous were now glad. But Shadrach, Meshach, and Abednego had faith. "Whatever you do," they said, "God can save us."

Dear God, I will only worship and obey You and no other thing. Amen.

DAY 222

Angel in the Fire

Daniel 3:19-25

The king was full of fury. Shadrach, Meshach, and Abednego would not pray to his statue of gold. So the king made sure the fire was extra hot. Then the three wise men were thrown into the fiery furnace. The king had to wipe his eyes when he looked. The three men were standing in the fire . . . not even hurt! And there was now four men in the fire. It was an angel who God had sent to protect them.

Dear God, Help me to obey You even when it is tough. Even if You don't take away hard things, I still will praise You. Amen.

DAY 223

The King Is Sure

Daniel 3:26-30

Shadrach, Meshach, and Abednego walked out of the fire. Not even one hair on their heads had been hurt! In fact, the three wise men did not even *smell* like smoke. The king and his princes could hardly believe it. It was settled then and there. The king had a new order. He said that no one was to say anything bad about God. "Because no one can save like God can," said the king. Then Shadrach, Meshach, and Abednego were made rulers.

Dear God, Thank You for saving me and that You keep saving me all the time. Amen.

Writing on the Wall

Daniel 5:1-29

The king was having a feast when God came to visit. The guests looked up because writing had appeared on the wall! The king was very afraid. He called for Daniel. Daniel would be able to tell him what the letters said. The news was not good. God was angry. The king had been too busy having fun to be good. So now, God was going to punish him. The sad king thanked Daniel for telling him the truth.

Dear God, Help me to have fun by doing what is right and not by leaving You. Amen.

DAY 225

Daniel in the Lions' Den

Daniel 6:7-23

There was a new rule that said for one month no one could pray to God but only to the king. Well, that was not a rule Daniel was going to obey. The king loved Daniel, but rules were rules. Daniel would have to be thrown into the den of lions. Yet Daniel had trust in God. Sure enough, God shut the lions' mouths. The king peeked in. Daniel was safe and sound. "Let us pray to the one true God!" cried the king.

Dear God, You saved Daniel from all the lions. That is amazing! Amen.

DAY 226

An Angel at the River

Daniel 10:4-12:10

One day Daniel saw an angel. The angel told Daniel about things that were going to happen. Kings would come, and huge nations would be built up. Other kings would try to take over. Some would lose; others would win and pretend to be God. "But the people who believe in the true God will be saved," the angel said to Daniel.

Dear God, You created angels to be Your workers who praise You and bring messages to Your people. Amen.

Joyful Thanks

Words of a Prophet. Isaiah 12:4-6

God is the one who will save me. That is why I will trust, and I will not be afraid. God is my strength and my song. That is why He will be welcomed with joy! Shout His name. Tell what God can do. Sing to God for all of the wonders He has done. Shout and sing, for God is great! And know that God lives with you.

DAY 228

The Capture

2 Chronicles 36:12-Ezra 1:3

The people of God had been taken to Babylon because they would not turn back to God. Eventually, the nation of Babylon was taken over by another nation called Persia. Now the people of Israel were servants of the Persians. But after many years, their hearts had finally turned back to God. One day the people of God heard some great news. The king of Persia was rich, and he wanted to help! He was going to give them whatever they needed to go and build a new house for God in Jerusalem.

Dear God, You never leave Your people and are ready
to give good things when we listen to You. Amen.

DAY 229

Call for a Queen

Esther 1:1-2:17

Esther lived in the land of Persia with her cousin. "Tell no one," he had said, "that we are from Israel." One day, a call came from the royal palace. The king of the land was looking for a queen. Royal servants gave each maiden one whole year of beauty treatments and special food. *Who is this beautiful maiden?* thought the king. When the king met Esther, his choice was made.

Dear God, Just like You made Esther the queen, You have a plan for me too. Amen.

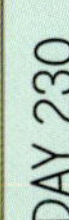

Esther Is Queen

Esther 2:17-18

No other maiden was like Esther, the king had decided. He put the royal crown on her head. Esther would be his wife. A great feast was held for the wedding of the king and Esther . . . now a queen.

Dear God, Whatever You ask me to do, help me do it with all my heart. Amen.

DAY 231

The Queen's Secret

Esther 4:4-8:16

Queen Esther had just heard some terrible news. An evil man called Haman planned to kill the Israelite people. That meant Esther . . . and Esther's whole family! She had to do something. She decided to be very brave. When the king saw his lovely queen, his heart filled with love. "Ask for anything," he said. So Esther told him her secret. She was from Israel. Would the king help? Of course he would! Esther had saved her people the Israelites.

Dear God, Wherever You put me, it is not an accident but on purpose. Help me to follow Your plan. Amen.

The Good Servant

Nehemiah 1:1-2:9

Nehemiah did not feel that he was anyone special. He was just a servant who poured the cup for the king of Persia. But Nehemiah was good and true, and he always smiled. So when he looked sad one day, the king was worried. Nehemiah told the king that things were not well at home. Would the king let Nehemiah make a visit to help Israel fix their broken city? The king agreed. He even sent his army to protect Nehemiah on the way.

Dear God, Whatever job I have, I will do it the best I can. Amen.

DAY 233

Turn to God

Words of a Prophet. Hosea 6:1-3

Come, and let us go back to God. We were torn, but He will heal us. We were broken, but He will fix us. He will raise us up to live always in His care. Let us keep on the path of God. Then we will know He is sure as morning. And God will come to us like rain that waters in both winter and in spring.

Dear God, Your love is like rain that makes me live and grow. Amen.

The Return

Ezra 1-3:11

The people of God were going home! In Israel they would build a brand new house for God. The king of Persia loaded them up with riches: animals to ride on and silver and gold to make God's house. When they got to Jerusalem, the people got to work. They cut wood. They laid stones for the floor. Then they all joined together to give thanks to God. "Because He is *good!*" they sang with a shout.

Dear God, You are good, and I want to always praise and honor You. Amen.

DAY 235

The City Healed

Nehemiah 2:11-6:19

Nehemiah made it home to Israel safe and sound. It was time to get to work, time to fix Jerusalem's wall. And all the men and women in Israel wanted to help. It was not long before the gates of the city rose up tall. When others came to make fun, the builders did not listen. Soon, the Sheep, Horse, and Fish Gates looked like new. The city looked almost like the war had never happened! The people were grateful to their leader Nehemiah.

Dear God, Help me be a good leader like Nehemiah who
helped people do what You asked them to do. Amen.

DAY 236

Windows of Love

Words of a Prophet. Malachi 3:1-12

God sees and knows everything. He will judge people who do wrong, hurt others, steal, and lie. Even still, He calls to His people saying, "Come back to me!" He will bless His people when they come back to worship Him. It will look like heaven opened a window and poured out good gifts.

Dear God, You judge the good and bad. You never change, and You pour out Your goodness. Amen.

The Wolf and Lamb

Words of a Prophet. Isaiah 65:17-25

"One day I will create a new heaven and earth," says God. "Celebrate and be glad. There will be no death, and I will answer my people before they finish praying. Even wolves and lambs will eat together in peace."

Dear God, In heaven everything will be perfect, and all people and animals will get along. How fun! Amen.

DAY 238

God on High

Words of a Prophet. Micah 4:1-4

One day, people from everywhere will come to God and start listening to what He says. They will no longer fight and go to war but live happily with each other. Weapons will no longer be used to hurt others but to dig and prune in the gardens. They will no longer be afraid but will enjoy life instead.

Dear God, I pray that people everywhere will come to know You and go to heaven. Amen.

A Child Will Come

Words of a Prophet. Isaiah 7:14; 9:6-7

When God sends his Son to earth, it will be like this: A young girl, who is not married, will become His mother, and she will call him Immanuel. Immanuel means God is with us. He will also be called Prince of Peace and Mighty God, our King forever.

Dear God, You told us about Jesus' coming a long time before he came. Thank You for Your amazing plan. Amen.

DAY 240

The Light of God

John 1:1-5

Jesus was with God in the beginning before anything else was made. Everything in heaven and on earth was made through Him. Without Him nothing would have been made. And in Him was life, the life that is the light of the world. The light shined into every dark place, and the darkness could not stop it.

Dear God, You were here from the beginning. Thank You for sending Your Son to show us the way. Amen.

DAY 241

Mary and the Angel

Luke 1:27-38

Mary was a young woman and not yet married. So when an angel visited, the message was surprising. "You are going to have a baby," said the angel to Mary. Mary said, "But how can I have a baby without a husband?" The angel answered, "The father of your baby is God. The baby shall be named Jesus, God's own Son." Mary trusted God. She was happy for the news. She told the angel, "May it happen just as you say."

Dear God, Mary trusted that no matter what would happen,
You would be with her. I want to trust You too. Amen.

DAY 242

Joseph's Visit

Matthew 1:20-25

The angel visited Joseph who was soon to be Mary's husband. "Mary's baby is the Son of God," the angel said. "You shall name him Jesus. He will save people from their sins." Joseph believed all the angel told him and prepared to be Jesus' dad here on earth.

Dear God, How wonderful that You sent an angel to tell Joseph about Jesus coming! Amen.

Name of Jesus

Matthew 1:22-23

Jesus would be called by many other names as well. The prophet Isaiah had written about Jesus long ago. Christ, the Son of God, would come to save the world. Jesus was also called Immanuel, which means God with us.

Dear God, You plan out history before it ever happens. You are always in control. Amen.

DAY 244

Mary and Elizabeth

Luke 1:39-55

Mary could hardly wait to tell her cousin Elizabeth the news. She was having a baby. Elizabeth was about to have a baby herself. When Elizabeth heard her cousin Mary at the door, the baby in Elizabeth's belly jumped for joy. "How glad my soul is in God!" said Mary to Elizabeth. "I was nobody important, but God took notice of me. He will help me and do what He promised. God surely is good to those who love Him."

Dear God, Growing up is getting me ready to do great things for You. Help me to do a good job. Amen.

Zecheriah

Luke 1:11-25, 57-64

An angel had told Elizabeth's husband about her baby. "But," Zechariah had said, "we are too old to have a baby!" "Very well," said the angel. "Because you don't believe, you will not be able to talk until baby John has come." Elizabeth's baby was born. Her relatives and neighbors wanted to name the baby Zechariah after his father, but Elizabeth said, "No, his name will be John." Then Zechariah took his pen and wrote, "His name is John." At that moment, Zechariah was able to speak again.

Dear God, Help me not to doubt that You can do anything even when it seems impossible. Amen.

The Call of John

Luke 1:65-80

People were amazed when Zechariah could talk again. Now they were sure that baby John was someone special. They did not yet know just how John would be special. But Zechariah did. The angel had told him. "You are going to be a prophet," Zechariah told his son. "You will teach and give light to those in darkness." John grew up strong in spirit and close to God. He went to live in the desert until the right time.

Dear God, You have amazing plans for Your people, and I want to be ready when You call. Amen.

DAY 247

The First Christmas

Luke 2:4-7

It was time. Jesus was ready to be born. Joseph led the donkey while Mary rode on its back. When they got to the inn, there was no more room. They would have to stay out with the animals instead. There in the animal stable, baby Jesus was born. Mary wrapped him up with swaddling clothes. They laid Jesus in a manger that was used to hold hay. Then they looked at baby Jesus, overflowing with love.

Dear God, Thank You for Jesus being born. That is why we celebrate Christmas! Amen.

Shepherds by Night

Luke 2:8-14

Some shepherds were watching their sheep at night when a light shone all around them. They were terrified. Then a voice said, "Fear not." It was an angel! "I bring you good news," said the angel. "Christ is born." Suddenly, there were even more angels there. The angels were praising God, saying, "Glory to God! Peace on Earth. May good come to those with whom God is pleased." The shepherds watched the angels in amazement.

Dear God, How exciting to see the angels singing in the sky! I want to sing about Jesus being born too. Amen.

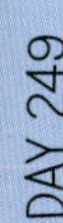

The Visitors

Luke 2:15-20

The angels that had visited the field went back to heaven. The shepherds looked at each other and said, "Let's go to Bethlehem and see this news for ourselves." Then they rushed to find Jesus. The shepherds found Mary and Joseph inside the stable. And there lay Jesus asleep on the hay in the manger. The shepherds could not wait to spread the exciting news. Then they praised God for all they had seen and heard.

Dear God, I am excited like the shepherds to tell everyone the good news of Jesus being born. Amen.

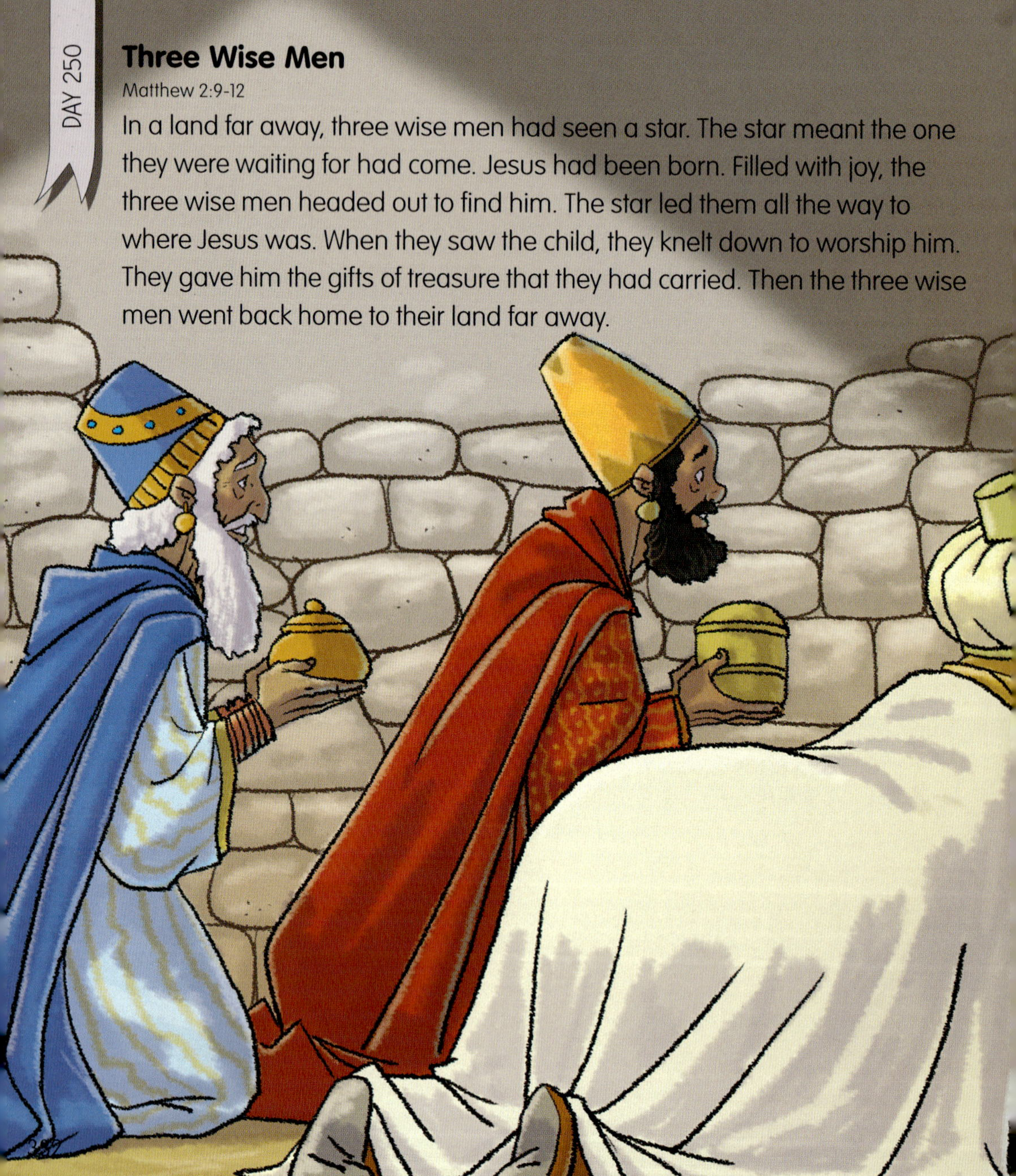

DAY 250

Three Wise Men

Matthew 2:9-12

In a land far away, three wise men had seen a star. The star meant the one they were waiting for had come. Jesus had been born. Filled with joy, the three wise men headed out to find him. The star led them all the way to where Jesus was. When they saw the child, they knelt down to worship him. They gave him the gifts of treasure that they had carried. Then the three wise men went back home to their land far away.

Dear God, Help me to give my best to You
and keep going wherever You lead me. Amen.

DAY 251

Simeon's Blessing

Luke 2:22-35

Joseph and Mary took Jesus to the temple in Jerusalem. They proudly showed their new baby to Simeon the priest. Simeon took him in his arms, saying, "Now my eyes have seen the light of the world!" Joseph and Mary listened to the priest with surprise; Simeon had already realized who Jesus really was! Then Simeon blessed Joseph, Mary, and baby Jesus. He said to Mary, "Now I have finally seen who will show us the way to God."

Dear God, You told Simeon who Jesus really
was. Thank You for telling me too. Amen.

DAY 252

The Prophet Anna

Luke 2:36-38

At the temple in Jerusalem lived a prophetess named Anna. She had prayed to God at the temple for many years. As soon as she saw Jesus, she knew—this was God's Son! Anna thanked God. She told everyone that Christ had come.

Dear God, Sometimes You ask us to wait, but Your promises always come true. Amen.

Jesus Grows

Luke 2:39-40

Joseph and Mary took Jesus home to the land of Galilee. Joseph was a carpenter in the city of Nazareth. Jesus would be taken care of by both Joseph and Mary. God was with him, and Jesus grew up strong and wise.

Dear God, Thank You for the people that take care of me. Amen.

DAY 254

A Boy Named Jesus

Luke 2:41-51

It was time to go home after their visit to Jerusalem. Joseph and Mary thought Jesus was right behind them. But when they looked, Jesus was nowhere to be seen. They rushed back and looked everywhere for the boy. There at last was Jesus talking to teachers and priests. His mother cried, "We have looked everywhere for you!" But He answered, "Didn't you know I had to be in my Father's house?"

Dear God, Jesus grew up as a child just like me,
but He knew all things because He is God. Amen.

DAY 255

John the Baptist

Mark 1:4-8

John ate foods from the wild. He dressed in leather and camel hair. John lived in the quietness of the wild and was a prophet of God. People came to see him at the river to tell him their sins. Afterward, John dipped them in the water to show their sins were washed away. John said, "I have baptized you with water. Yet someone with even more power than me is going to come." The church leaders wanted to know who John really was. John said, "I am not God's son . . . but He is coming soon."

Dear God, Help me to be like John
and tell others about You. Amen.

DAY 256

John Teaches

Luke 3:2-11

John went around to share God's Word. John was making the world ready to meet Jesus just like the prophets of long ago had said that he would. People came to John to be baptized and to hear him teach. They asked, "What must we do to get saved by God?" John told them, "If you have two coats, give one away. If you have food, then share your food as well."

Dear God, I want to know your Word so I can
tell others what You want them to hear. Amen.

DAY 257

The Baptism

Matthew 3:13-17

Jesus left Galilee and went to the Jordan River to have his cousin John baptize him. As Jesus rose from the water, God's Spirit came down from heaven like a dove, and it shone on him. Then a voice out of heaven said, "This is my beloved Son. I delight in Him."

Dear God, Thank You for sending
Jesus here to tell us about You. Amen.

DAY 258

The Desert

Mark 1:12-13; Matthew 4:1-11

After he was baptized, Jesus went into the wilderness. He stayed alone among the wild animals for forty days. There, the devil tried to get Jesus to do something wrong. But Jesus kept God in his heart and did not make a bad choice.

Dear God, Protect me from what is evil, and help me to know that You are always with me. Amen.

The Call of Jesus

Mark 1:14-20

Jesus left the desert and went into Galilee along the sea. As he went, Jesus told people about the Kingdom of God. God was ready to welcome them to a life of peace and joy. All they had to do was believe and stop doing wrong. Soon Jesus saw some fishermen at work with their nets. Jesus said to them, "Follow me, and I'll show you how to catch people instead of fish." Each fisherman left his ship and followed after Jesus. Simon, Andrew, James, and John were now disciples.

Dear God, I believe in You and want to turn away from my bad choices. Thank You for forgiving me and saving me. Amen.

DAY 260

The Wedding Feast

John 2:1-11

Jesus and his disciples were asked to come to a wedding. Mary was glad to see her son arrive because there was a problem. The wedding ran out of wine, but Mary knew Jesus could help. Jesus told the servants to fill all the pitchers with water. When the servants poured it out into the cups—the water had turned into wine! It was the best wine anyone had ever tasted. With that, the miracles of Jesus had now begun. Jesus showed his power, and his disciples believed in him.

Dear God, Jesus did amazing miracles! Thank you for showing us You care for all our needs. Amen.

DAY 261

Nicodemus and Jesus

John 3:1-8

One night a man named Nicodemus came to visit Jesus. He wanted to know if Jesus was really from God and was God. Jesus told him, "If the Spirit of God changes you, he will make you new from the inside. Only then can you believe in me and be my true follower."

Dear God, Thank You that I can be born again as Your child when I believe in You. Amen.

Son of God

John 3:16-17

"God loved the world so very much," said Jesus, "that He gave His only Son so that those who believe in me will have life forever and ever with God in Heaven. God sent His Son into the world, not to tell people how bad they are . . . but to save people."

Dear God, When I believe in You, I will live forever with You in Heaven! Amen.

DAY 263

Woman at the Well

John 4:7-29

One day Jesus met a Samaritan woman at a well. Samaritans and Jews were not good friends. The Jews would not even speak to the Samaritans. But Jesus spoke kindly to the woman asking her for water. "Why are you speaking to me?" the woman asked. Jesus said, "I don't only want to speak with you but to give you a gift, a gift better than cold water on a hot day. My gift is eternal life." The woman looked puzzled. She did not quiet understand. "If you believe in me," Jesus said, "you will have eternal life. I can give this to you—because I am the Son of God."

Dear God, You want to give us eternal life as
a gift when we believe in You. Amen.

DAY 264

Through the Roof

Luke 5:18-26

The friends of a sick man had a plan to get to Jesus. But the house was too full to get through the door. So they sent their friend down through the roof. Very gently, they lowered the sick man into the house. Jesus was amazed—what good friends this man had! Jesus said, "Your sins are forgiven. Get up, take up your mat, and go home." And right away, the man was healed. The man got up and thanked God the whole way home. And everyone in the house knew that God was great.

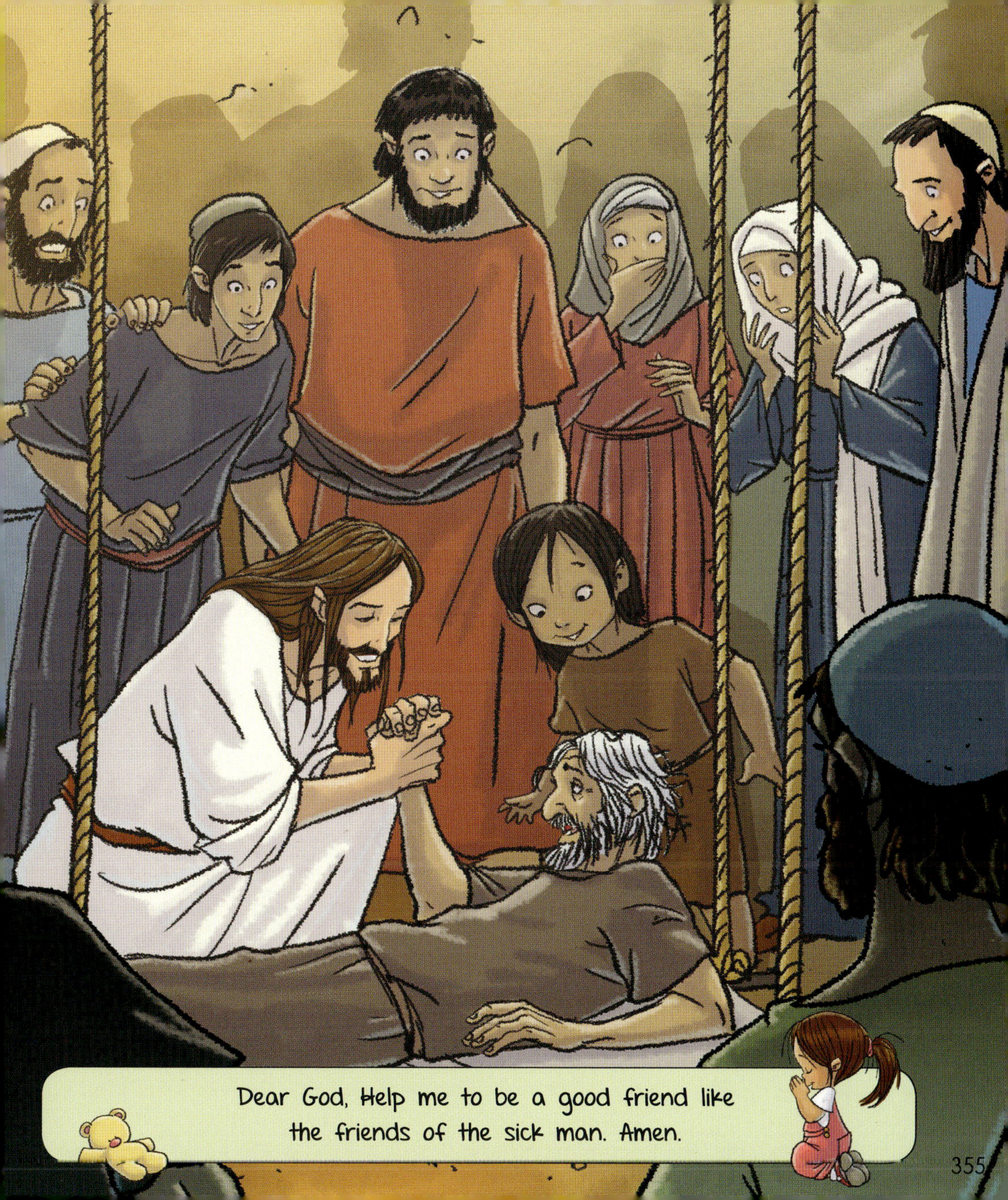
Dear God, Help me to be a good friend like
the friends of the sick man. Amen.

DAY 265

The Pool

John 5:1-17

A sick man was lying next to the pool of healing water. He was too sick to get into the pool by himself. When Jesus saw the man, he said, "Rise, and walk." The man was healed without even stepping into the water. What Jesus did made some of the Jews very angry. Jesus had healed the man on the holy day, and the law said that nobody could work on that day. Jesus answered that God worked *every day*, and so did he.

Dear God, You ask us to rest from regular work one day a week, but we should still help and serve others everyday. Amen.

DAY 266

Jesus on a Mountain

Matthew 4:25-5:16

People from all over wanted to hear what Jesus had to say. He and his disciples went town to town telling about God. When he left town to go up a mountain, a crowd followed. So at the top of the mountain, Jesus sat and began to teach. "You are the light of the world," Jesus told the people. "No one lights a candle only to hide it away. A candle is lit to light up where it is dark. Let your light shine by doing what is good."

Dear God, I want my love for You to shine like a candle and not be hidden. Amen.

Blessed Are You

Matthew 5:2-9

Jesus was teaching people about what would make them truly happy. What he said was like nothing they had ever heard before. He didn't say that the strong and smart would be the happy ones. And He didn't say that the rich and popular would be the happiest either. No, He said that those who are poor and weak would be the happy ones. They would be happy because they would need his powerful help instead of trying on their own.

Dear God, Thank You that when I feel weak or alone, You are right beside me helping me out. Amen.

Birds and Flowers

A Story Jesus Told. Matthew 6:24-30

Serve God and only God. Then, don't worry what you will eat or drink. Don't worry how healthy you are. Don't worry what you are going to wear. Look up instead. Watch the birds that fly. God feeds them, so won't He also then feed you? Think about the flowers and how beautiful they grow. God dresses them, so won't He also dress you?

Dear God, You don't want us to worry about anything that we need. Help me to trust in You. Amen.

How to Pray

Matthew 6:9-13

Jesus told the people, "When you pray, pray like this: Our Father in heaven, holy is Your name. May Your kingdom come. May Your will be done on earth just like it is in Heaven. Give us today our daily bread. Forgive our sins as we have forgiven others. Keep us from doing wrong. Keep us from harm. For yours is the kingdom and power and glory forever. Amen."

Dear God, You want us to pray to You,
so I will do that every day. Amen.

DAY 270

The Tree

Matthew 7:15-23

Watch out for people who say one thing but do another. They might say the right things, but when it comes to doing it, they don't. Anyone who says they know me and follow me should love God and others, too. So notice what people do more than what they say. That way you will know who really knows the truth. It is like a fruit tree. You can pick good fruit from a good tree, but a bad tree only leaves you with bad fruit or no fruit at all.

Dear God, What people do shows if they are good or bad.
Help me to do good things to show people You. Amen.

DAY 271

The Builders

Luke 6:46-49

Jesus told the people, "Hear what I say. Then, do what I tell you to do. That way you will be like a house built on rock. The house on a rock will not shake in a storm. But any who do not obey my lessons are like a house built on sand. When a storm comes, the house shakes. And soon the house is washed away."

Dear God, I will build my life on Your word so it will be strong. Amen.

Jesus Heals

Matthew 8:1-13

Wherever Jesus and his disciples went, people followed. A sick man came saying, "Lord, you can make me well." Jesus touched him, and the man was better right away. So others came. And Jesus made them well, one by one.

Dear God, You made me and know everything about me. Amen.

DAY 273

What is Faith?

Luke 7:1-10

Some people were rushing toward Jesus. The favorite servant of their friend was about to die. Would Jesus come to help? When the man saw Jesus coming, he stopped him. Sure, the man was rich. He had many servants and friends. But he didn't feel important enough to bother Jesus. "Still," said the man, "I know you can heal my servant with just a word." Jesus was filled with joy. This man had faith! Back at the house, the man's servant was found to be perfectly well again.

Dear God, I have faith that You are God
and are the most powerful. Amen.

DAY 274

Jesus Answers

Matthew 11:3-6

Long ago, the prophets wrote that Christ would come. Now some disciples wanted to know if Jesus was the Christ. Jesus answered that his miracles proved that he indeed was. Jesus told them, "Go and share what you have seen me do. The blind can now see; the crippled can now walk," Jesus said. "The sick are made well, and the deaf can hear. The dead are raised up, and the poor learn about God. And whoever believes in me, they will be blessed."

Dear God, You told us that Jesus was coming, and when He came He said He was God's Son. Amen.

Mary Magdalene

Luke 8:1-3

Mary Magdalene was not well at all. Then she met Jesus. Mary believed in Jesus with all her heart. Jesus healed her and they became good friends. Mary even gave a lot of what she had to help Jesus and his disciples when they traveled around Israel.

DAY 276

The Mustard Seed

A Story Jesus Told. Mark 4:30-32

The Kingdom of Heaven is like a tiny seed of a mustard plant. It is the smallest of all seeds. But when it is planted, it grows into the tallest of all of the plants in the garden. And birds come to rest in its shade.

Dear God, You came to earth as a tiny baby, but now many people know You all over the world! Amen.

DAY 277

The Pearl

A Story Jesus Told. Matthew 13:45-46

The Kingdom of Heaven is like the perfect pearl to a man looking for good pearls. When he found one that was perfect, the cost didn't matter. He was happy giving everything he had so he could get it.

Dear God, No matter what it takes or what it costs, I want to love You always. Amen.

DAY 278

The Net

A Story Jesus Told. Matthew 13:47-49

The Kingdom of Heaven is like a net thrown into the sea. When the net got pulled up, it held every kind of fish. The good fish were kept. The bad were tossed back. Just like this, when the end comes, the angels will separate the good people from the bad people.

Dear God, Everyone who believes in You is called good, and You will take them to Heaven where You are. Amen.

Jesus on the Sea

Mark 4:35-38

It had been a long day in Galilee. Jesus had healed many, and Jesus had fed many. Now it was almost dark. Time to set sail. Jesus and his disciples got in their boat to cross the sea. A storm started to form over the water. But Jesus didn't worry. He knew that God was always with him. So he just fell sound asleep on his pillow. The disciples were afraid though. How could Jesus be sleeping in a storm like this?

Dear God, Even when a storm is coming, I feel safe because You are with me. Amen.

DAY 280

Jesus Stops the Storm

Mark 4:37-40

The storm was growing stronger and stronger. The waves crashed. The sky howled. The disciples no longer felt brave. They ran to wake Jesus. "Master," cried a disciple, "we are about to drown!" Jesus got up and said, "Peace, be still!" Then the storm stopped. Everything grew calm and quiet. Jesus said to his disciples, "Why were you afraid?" Jesus knew God was there protecting them no matter what.

Dear God, I will not be afraid because
You can make any storm stop! Amen.

The Sick Girl

Mark 5:22-24; Luke 8:40-42

Jairus was an important man in town. Many of his friends didn't like Jesus, but Jairus respected Jesus and believed Jesus had power. One day Jairus' only daughter became very, very sick. So Jairus went to find Jesus. "My daughter is so sick that she might die," Jairus told him. Jesus agreed to help and got up to go with Jairus to his house.

Dear God, You are always ready to help those
in need. Help me to do that too. Amen.

The Woman's Faith

Mark 5:25-34

Jesus stopped suddenly. "Who touched me?" he said. A frightened-looking woman stepped forward. "I was sick for years, but touching your robe healed me!" Jesus smiled. "Because you believed I could heal you, you are healed!" he said.

Dear God, Help me to keep trying and not give up and to know that You will be with me. Amen.

DAY 283

The Lost Child

Mark 5:35-39; Luke 8:49-53

A servant ran out to meet Jesus and Jairus as they walked. The servant had bad news. It was too late for Jesus to help. The little daughter of Jairus had already died. But Jesus said to Jairus, "Don't worry; only believe." Jesus and three disciples went into Jairus' house. Friends and family were gathered, weeping with sadness. Jesus looked down at the little girl laying on the bed. "Don't worry," Jesus said. "She's not dead . . . only sleeping."

Dear God, Even when something seems hopeless and impossible, I will believe You can work it out. Amen.

The Girl Awakes

Mark 5:39-42; Luke 8:52-55

The girl had died, but Jesus said she was just sleeping. *What was Jesus thinking?* the people thought. And now Jesus was looking down at the girl and taking her hand saying, "Little girl, get up." The girl's eyes fluttered. Then she sat straight up. Her family and friends could hardly believe their eyes! Jesus had brought the little girl back from the dead. Her father and mother thanked Jesus through tears of joy.

Dear God, I never want to doubt You because You can do anything! Amen.

DAY 285

The Boy's Gift

Matthew 14:15-21

Jesus was teaching a crowd in the desert. It grew late. His friends said, "There is no food for the people to eat." Just then, a small boy stepped out of the crowd. "I have two fish and five loaves of bread," said the boy. Jesus took the boy's gift. Jesus prayed a blessing on it. Then He started to break the fish and bread in pieces. More and more, more and more. There was so much food that the whole crowd stuffed their bellies full!

Walking on Water

John 6:17-20

It was a dark and stormy night on the sea. The disciples wished Jesus was with them, but he was spending alone time on a mountain. They looked out across the dark, wild waves. Then they saw it, a man walking on the water! He was coming straight toward them. They were terrified. Then the man on the water spoke with a voice they knew. "Do not be afraid," said Jesus. "It is I."

Dear God, I will not be afraid when there are storms because You are always with me in the storm. Amen.

DAY 287

Peter Steps Out

Matthew 14:28-32

The disciples were amazed to see Jesus walking on the sea. "If it's really you," said Peter, "then let me come out there." Jesus agreed, so Peter climbed over the edge of the boat. He stretched out his foot. Peter could walk on water too! Then Peter saw the storm all around him. He became afraid. Peter crashed down into the water. Jesus came to help. "Why did you not trust me?" said Jesus as he pulled Peter out. Jesus helped Peter onto the boat, and the storm stopped.

Dear God, You have power over all the
Earth and can even walk on water! Amen.

DAY 288

The Bread

John 6:35-38

"I am the bread of life," said Jesus to the people. "Whoever comes to me, they will never go hungry. Whoever believes in me, they will never thirst. Whoever loves me, I will love."

What Peter Knows

Matthew 16:15-17

One day Jesus asked his disciples, "Who am I?" Peter answered right away, "You are Christ, the Son of God." Jesus smiled. "Bless you, Peter," said Jesus. "You listened to no one but God and what he told your heart."

Dear God, Thank You for showing me that Jesus is Your Son who came to save us. Amen.

DAY 290

The Lamp on a Stand

A Story Jesus Told. Luke 8:16-18

No one goes and turns on a light then hides the light under the bed. They put the light out on a table so that everyone can see where it had been dark before. "There are many secrets on this earth. But light will be shined wherever secrets hide. So listen carefully to understand. Do what is wise, and more wise you will be."

Dear God, Help me be a light in a dark world to lead people to Your truth. Amen.

Jesus Shines

Matthew 17:1-9

Jesus took three of his friends up a high mountain. When they reached the top, something happened. Jesus started to shine right before their eyes. He lit up like a bright, white light. A bright cloud floated over them, and a voice said, "This is my beloved Son whom I delight in. Listen to him." His friends hid their faces, but Jesus said not to be afraid. Then they all went back down the mountain.

Dear God, Jesus was a human being and God all at the same time because He is Your Son. Amen.

Jesus and the Child

Luke 9:46-48

The disciples of Jesus were not looking too happy. They were fighting over which one of them was the greatest. Jesus heard them. He called a child nearby to come over. Then he sat the child down right by his side. Jesus had an answer for his friends on who was greatest. "Do you see this child?" Jesus said to the disciples. "Whoever will welcome this child, will welcome God. Because to God the greatest is the one who is small."

Dear God, Help me not to try to be first and always the most important but to think about other people. Amen.

DAY 293

The Feast

John 7:11-16

The people at the feast wondered where Jesus was. They talked about him quietly while they waited. "Jesus is a good man," said some. "No," said others, "he doesn't tell the truth." There in the middle of the feast came Jesus to teach. The leaders had started to become suspicious. "How does Jesus know so much about God?" some of them asked. He had not been taught like they had. Jesus answered, "What I teach comes from God not me."

Dear God, Put Your words in my mouth
so that all I say comes from You. Amen.

DAY 294

The Help of Nicodemus

John 7:42-53

The people in charge had enough. They did not like how Jesus made new rules. They did not want people to obey Jesus instead of them. They wanted to put Jesus in jail. "Wait!" said a voice. It was ruler Nicodemus. "We can't put a man in jail for no good reason," said Nicodemus. "It says so in our very own law." And he was right. So the others left Jesus alone and went home.

Dear God, I want to believe in You even when others don't, so please give me courage. Amen.

Jesus Forgives

John 8:1-11

A crowd of people was making a lot of noise. "This woman has done wrong," they cried to Jesus. "Very well," Jesus replied. "Whoever of you has never done a wrong thing," he said, "can punish her." Then Jesus kneeled and wrote in the sand. When he looked up again, the crowd had all gone away. "No one was perfect?" Jesus said to the woman. "Go along, and sin no more."

Dear God, Thank You for Your forgiveness because no one but You is perfect. Help me to forgive others. Amen.

DAY 296

The Good Shepherd

A Story Jesus Told. John 10:11-19

A shepherd who is good will give his life for his sheep. A shepherd who is bad will see a wolf and run away. The wolf comes for the sheep and makes them scatter. The bad shepherd cares about himself and not his sheep. I am like the good shepherd. I know all my sheep. And all my sheep know who I am as well. My Father sent me to call for any sheep that might be lost. He loves me because I give my life for the sheep.

Dear God, You know all about me, and You love me like a shepherd cares for his sheep. Amen.

The Disciples

Luke 10:1-11

Jesus told his disciples to share God's love far and wide. He said, "Whomever you meet, greet them with peace. Then if someone doesn't like you, don't be sad. Brush it off like dirt on your shoes."

Dear God, I want to bring peace and not fighting to my family and friends. Amen.

DAY 298

The Good Stranger

A Story Jesus Told. Luke 10:30-37

A man on his way to town was robbed. The robbers took all that he had then left him in the dirt. Soon a priest walked by. But he did not stop to help. A person from town walked by. He did not help either. Then a stranger from far away came by and stopped. He picked the hurt man up off the ground. Then he carried him to the hospital and paid for his bill. This is what it means to love: helping whoever is in need.

Dear God, I never want to be too busy to help others
or to give what I have to people in need. Amen.

The Friend

A Story Jesus Told. Luke 11:5-13

Pretend you go to your friend's house late one night. You ask to borrow some bread because you ran out. Will your friend say, "Go away; I'm in bed"? No, a friend will get out of bed if you need help. It's the same way with God, your Father in Heaven. Ask—and what you want will be given to you. Seek—and you will find what you are looking for. Knock—and the door will be opened for you.

Dear God, When I ask to know You and seek to find You, You are always ready to give me help. Amen.

The Rich Fool

A Story Jesus Told. Luke 12:16-33

A rich farmer didn't know where to put all his crops. Then he said, "I know! I'll build bigger barns to save it in. That way I can just relax for many years." But he died before he got to enjoy what he had saved. That's what happens to those who save riches on earth instead of working to be rich with God. So give to the poor. Then you'll save treasure in heaven. Treasure in heaven never gets stolen or destroyed.

Dear God, Help me not want to have a lot of riches here on earth but to obey You and have riches in Heaven. Amen.

DAY 301

A Good Servant

A Story Jesus Told. Luke 12:35-40

Be ready to serve God every single minute. Keep your light always burning bright. Keep watch for God through the window of your heart. That way when He knocks, you can open up right away. A master is proud of a servant who is ready, and the master will always take care of the servant too. To serve God, you yourself must always be ready. You never know just when God is going to knock.

Dear God, I want to always be ready to serve You so I
will keep watch for what You want me to do. Amen.

The Lost Coin

A Story Jesus Told. Luke 15:8-10

A woman had lost one of her ten special silver coins. She searched her house all over until she found it. Then she called her friends to celebrate the happy news. Like this, the angels celebrate each time a lost person believes in Jesus and says I'm sorry for making bad choices.

Dear God, You celebrate every time a person believes in You. Help me to be brave and tell others about You. Amen.

DAY 303

The Lost Son

A Story Jesus Told. Luke 15:10-20

A man had saved some money for his two sons to inherit. The younger son said, "Father, I want my money now." Then he left home and wasted all his money. At last he ran out of money. The son started to get hungry. He went back home very, very sad because of all the foolish things he had done. Yet to his surprise, his father wasn't angry with him; he was just glad his son was home. And so it is with your Father in Heaven. Turn away from doing wrong, and God will forgive you.

Dear God, Keep my heart and my mind from wandering away from You. Amen.

Lazarus Sleeps

John 11:7-25

One day Jesus said to his disciples, "Let's go to our friend Lazarus' house. Lazarus has died, but I am going to wake him up again." When they arrived, Lazarus had already been dead for four days. Jesus told Lazarus' sister Martha, "Your brother will wake up to life again." Martha answered, "I know he will rise to go to heaven." Jesus said, "Believe in me, and even the dead will live."

Dear God, Help me to obey You even when it might be uncomfortable or dangerous. Amen.

DAY 305

Jesus Weeps

John 11:28-37

Martha's sister Mary learned that Jesus had come. She ran to see him. "If you had been here," cried Mary, "then my brother Lazarus would not have died." Seeing Mary cry made Jesus terribly sad. Jesus asked to be taken to where Lazarus was. When he saw the grave of his good friend, Jesus cried. Some said, "Look how much Jesus loved Lazarus!" But others said, "Could Jesus not save his own friend?"

Lazarus Rises

John 11:38-44

Jesus was upset over the death of his friend Lazarus. He said to those at the grave, "Take the stone away." "But Lord," Martha said, "he's been dead for four days!" Jesus said to Martha, "Didn't I tell you to believe?" The grave stone was rolled away. Jesus prayed to God, thanking Him for the miracle God was about to do. Then Jesus cried out, "Lazarus, come out of there!" Lazarus rose up just as if he had never even been dead.

Dear God, I believe You can do all things like make Lazarus alive again after he was dead. Amen.

Ten Sick Men

Luke 17:12-14

Jesus was going through a village when he heard crying. "Jesus, Master, help us!" cried ten very sick-looking men. Jesus answered, "Go and show yourselves to the priest. He will know if you are well again." They turned to obey. And as they went, all ten were healed.

Dear God, You can heal any sickness because
You are in control of everything. Amen.

DAY 308

Thanks of One

Luke 17:15-19

One of the ten sick men was from a different country. When the foreigner looked down at his body, he had been healed! He turned back to find Jesus, praising God as he went. At the feet of Jesus, the man bowed down in thanks. Jesus looked down. "I thought ten were healed," he said. "Where are the other nine men?" But only the stranger had come back to thank Jesus. "Arise," Jesus said to him. "Your faith has made you well."

Dear God, You give me so many blessings. I want to always be grateful and say Thank You. Amen.

Jesus and the Children

Mark 10:13-16

Everyone wanted to get close to Jesus. They crowded around. The disciples tried to send all the children away, but Jesus stopped them. "Don't send them away! Let the children come to me," said Jesus. He picked the children up in his arms, and he blessed them.

Dear God, You always welcome the children to
come to You. Thank You for loving me. Amen.

The Young Ruler

Mark 10:17-21

A rich young man ran after Jesus. "Good Master!" he called. Jesus stopped, and the young man bowed down on his knee. "What do I have to do," said the man, "to get eternal life? I already follow all of God's commandments." Jesus looked down at the young man with love. "There is only one thing you are missing," said Jesus. "Give all you have to the poor, and follow me. Then your treasure will be in heaven."

Dear God, I never want the things I have to be more important than following You with all my heart. Amen.

Camel Through a Needle

Mark 10:22-27

The young man was very unhappy. Jesus had just told him to give his riches to the poor! Didn't Jesus know how much all his nice things had cost? He walked away feeling awful and sad. Jesus turned to those around him. "How hard it is," Jesus said, "for the rich to enter the Kingdom of God. It is easier for a camel to go through the eye of a needle. Yet even still," said Jesus, "nothing is impossible for God."

Dear God, I am so happy that nothing is impossible for You. You can do anything. Amen.

DAY 312

Zacchaeus in a Tree

Luke 19:1-5

Zacchaeus was very short. He was also very rich. Zacchaeus took money from others that was not his. One day Jesus came to Jericho. Everyone wanted to see Jesus—even tiny Zacchaeus. Zacchaeus had to climb up a tree in order to see. When Jesus walked by the tree, he stopped and looked up. "Zacchaeus, come down," said Jesus. "I'm coming to eat at your house today."

Dear God, You always forgive me and love me no matter what, just like You did for Zacchaeus. Amen.

DAY 313

Lost and Found

Luke 19:6-10

Of all the people in Jericho, Jesus had picked Zacchaeus—a man that everyone knew did wrong! Zacchaeus scrambled down the tree and ran to Jesus. He was filled with joy that Jesus wanted to be his friend. "Lord," said Zacchaeus, "I will give half my riches to the poor. And anything I stole, I will give the person back even more." Jesus could see Zacchaeus was sorry and forgave him.

Dear God, When I love You with my whole heart, I want to do what is right and serve others. Amen.

The Precious Oil

Matthew 26:6-13; Mark 14:3-9; John 12:2-8

Jesus was eating dinner at Simon's house when Mary came in. She stooped in front of Jesus. Then she opened her special jar of expensive perfume and wiped his feet with her hair. "Jesus," said his unhappy friend, "this woman is wasting perfume that we could have sold for the poor." But Jesus smiled down. "Leave her alone," he said. "She is doing a wonderful thing. You will always have the poor, but you will not always have me here."

Dear God, You are more important than my most special treasure. I love You more than anything that I have. Amen.

A Donkey for Jesus

Matthew 21:1-7

Two friends had a special job. Jesus had told them where to find a donkey with her foal. "Untie them," Jesus said, "and bring them here." The two men found the donkey and foal right where Jesus had said they would be. They told the owner Jesus needed them. "No problem at all," said the owner. So the two men took the donkeys. From their clothes, they made a saddle. Jesus was going to ride on the donkey into Jerusalem.

Dear God, You have a special plan and make all things happen in a special way. Amen.

The Road of Jesus

Matthew 21:8-11

Jesus was coming to Jerusalem! People from all around came to the road. They laid their clothes down for his donkey to walk on . . . just like anyone should do for a king. "Hosanna!" they cried, waving leaves from a palm tree. As Jesus came into Jerusalem, the city was curious. "Who is this?" they asked. The people who had followed after Jesus cried out, "It is Jesus, the prophet of Galilee!"

Dear God, Just like a king used to do, Jesus rode a donkey into the city because Jesus is the real King. Amen.

The Tables Turn

Matthew 21:12-13

The people looked up. An angry-looking man had just burst into the temple. *Crash* went a booth as the man flipped over the table. All the seller's glittery trinkets hit the floor. "God's house is not a place to buy and sell but a place to pray and worship," shouted the man. It was Jesus. *Crash* went the next booth. *Ring, ting* went the coins bouncing on the stone.

Dear God, I will treat Your house as a special place where we come to worship You and be with other Christians. Amen.

A Mountain of Faith

Matthew 21:18-22

Jesus was hungry. He saw a fig tree and went to check it out. There was no fruit on the tree only leaves. Jesus said, "May this tree never grow fruit again." His friends knew better than to ignore what Jesus said. They watched the tree shrivel and die right then and there. Jesus saw his friends were impressed. "If you just have faith," Jesus told them, "then you, too, can move even a mountain. Just pray, and believe, and anything you ask for will happen."

Dear God, Give me faith to believe that anything I ask for in Your name according to Your plan, You will do. Amen.

DAY 319

Two Children

A Story Jesus Told. Matthew 21:28-32

Two sons got a chore. The first son said no thanks; he did not want to go pick grapes. Then he realized that was wrong, so he went and picked grapes like his father had said. The other son said yes . . . at first. Then he decided that it didn't sound like much fun. He did not obey after all. So which son did what was right? The one who knew that he was wrong and made a change.

Dear God, Show me when I am wrong
and help me do the right thing. Amen.

The Last Supper

John 14; Matthew 26:26-30

"It's almost time for me to go," said Jesus at supper. His friends looked at one another with sad faces. "Yet still," Jesus told them, "I will be with you even when you can't see me." Jesus broke bread for them to eat and then passed his cup for all to have a sip. "Keep my words inside your heart," Jesus said. "Then in your heart, I will always be." They ate their last bread together and sang a song. Then Jesus told them to stand. It was time for them to go, so God's will could be done.

Dear God, When I see the special bread and drink at church, I will remember the Last Supper and Your love for me. Amen.

DAY 321

The Way Home

John 14:1-6

"Let not your heart be sad," Jesus said to his friends. "Trust in God and trust in me too. In my Father's house there are many mansions. And I am going there now to make a place for you." Thomas said, "But how will we know the way, Lord?" Jesus told them, "I am the Way, the Truth, and the Life. No one comes to the Father except through me."

Dear God, Believing in Jesus is the way to Heaven
where You are making a place for me. Amen.

The Vine

A Story Jesus Told. John 15:1-8

I am like the vine. My Father is like the gardener, and you are like the branches. Every branch that grows no fruit, my Father takes away. Every branch that has fruit, He cleans it up so it will grow more fruit. If you stay close to me like I stay close to you, you will grow much fruit and not wither. When you stay close to me and remember my words in your heart, then ask me for anything, and it will be done for you. It brings joy to God's heart when he sees that you bear much fruit.

Dear God, I will always be attached to You like the branch is to the vine so that I can grow lots of fruit. Amen.

Be Glad Always

John 16

Jesus told his disciples what was soon going to happen. "I am going away," He said, "back to my Father." The disciples would not see him for a while, but then he would come back again. Jesus told his friends, "I say these things to give you peace in your heart. Out there in the world, you will have troubles. But be happy knowing that I have already won!"

Dear God, I am so happy that when I have trouble, You will help me win since You have already won. Amen.

DAY 324

Jesus in the Garden

Matthew 26:36-56

After supper, Jesus prayed in a garden. He and his friends were turning to go when they suddenly stopped. Men with swords were coming straight for Jesus. And who led the way but the disciple Judas. Peter, another disciple of Jesus, drew his sword. "Put that away," Jesus ordered. "This is what must be." Then the soldiers took Jesus, and he was gone.

Dear God, Jesus followed Your plan even when
it was hard. Help me to do that to. Amen.

DAY 325

The Rooster Crows

Matthew 26:31-35,69-75; John 18:15-27

"It can't be true," Peter had said. "I won't let them take you away." But Jesus had told Peter, "Even before the rooster crows in the morning, you will have lied saying you don't know me." Now Jesus had been taken. Peter stood by a fire getting warm. "Hey you," said a soldier, "I saw you with Jesus, right?" Peter answered, "Jesus? I don't even know him." Just then, *cock-a-doodle-doo*. The rooster made Peter remember. Jesus had been right. Peter was too afraid to act like a friend.

Dear God, Sometimes it is scary to show others
I know You. Help me be brave. Amen.

DAY 326

The Price for the World

Matthew 27:26-54

It had been decided. Jesus was going to be nailed to a cross. They stuck a crown of thorns on his head and put him high on a hill. Jesus felt the hurt. He was bleeding, and his friends had gone away. Jesus felt alone. And he was going to die. But Jesus had decided to die all along. He was praying for the sins of the world to be forgiven. He was dying so that the world could be saved. Jesus looked up to God one last time; then he shut his eyes.

Dear God, You sent Your Son to die so
I could be saved. Thank You! Amen.

DAY 327

The Rich Friend

Matthew 27:55-61

Mary Magdalene and Mary, James' mother, hung their heads. Jesus had died. Then they got some good news. A rich man named Joseph paid the money to bury Jesus in his own tomb. Joseph wrapped Jesus in clean cloths and laid him in a cave that was cut out for a tomb.

Dear God, I will give whatever I have
so it can be used for You. Amen.

DAY 328

Guards at the Cave

Matthew 27:62-66

Jesus had died the day before. Yet the teachers of the law were starting to worry. What was it Jesus had said . . . that he would rise from the dead? *Better to be safe than sorry,* thought the teachers. They made sure the cave was closed tight with a huge rock in front. Then they put soldiers to stand guard. "Who could get in or out of a cave like that?" said the teachers.

Dear God, No matter what anyone does, Your plans will happen because You are mighty. Amen.

The Angel and the Stone

Luke 24:1-4; Matthew 28:1-4

Mary and Mary Magdalene woke up early. They were going to visit the cave where Jesus was buried. They headed out just as the sun was starting to rise. As they got to the cave, the ground started to shake. What was happening? It was an angel rolling away the giant rock that covered up the tomb. As the dust cleared, the women looked around. There lay the two guards who had been standing watch, and the angel was sitting on the rock.

Dear God, You send Your angels to do amazing things like when an angel rolled away the stone! Amen.

DAY 330

Jesus is Alive

Matthew 28:5-8; Luke 24:5-10

The angel's face shone like lightening. His clothes were white as snow. From his seat on the rock, the angel looked down at the women. "Don't be afraid," said the angel. "I know you came because of Jesus, but he is not here." The women listened as still as statues. The angel smiled. "Jesus is risen," he said. "Go see for yourself." Sure enough, no one was in the cave. The women felt full of fear and joy all at once! They ran to tell the news.

Dear God, Wow, Jesus was dead and then came
to life again. He isn't dead anymore! Amen.

DAY 331

The Risen Jesus

Matthew 28:8-10

The women had talked to an angel. Now, they were running down the road. They had to tell what they saw right away. But who was this standing in their way? It was Jesus! The women fell down at his feet, bursting with love. "Tell the others," said Jesus, "that they will see me soon as well."

Dear God, Help me to always be ready to tell
others that You are alive. Jesus is alive! Amen.

The Women Tell the Truth

Luke 24:9-12

Joanna went with Mary and Mary Magdalene to tell the others that Jesus was alive. Joanna and her friends burst into the house. They told all about the angel that said Jesus was alive and then about seeing Jesus himself. But the others didn't believe it and thought what the women said was all nonsense. Peter wasn't sure though. So he got up to go see for himself.

Dear God, I pray for others to know that You are alive and to believe in You. Amen.

Peter Goes to See

John 20:3-10

Peter and one of the other disciples had run the whole way to the cave. Now Peter stepped in. The light was dim inside the cave. Peter looked around. He saw a pile of white cloth and the special cloth that had been laid over Jesus' face. But Jesus himself was not to be seen. He had been taken somewhere, and His body was gone. There was nothing for them to do about it. So they left the cave and went home.

Dear God, When I am confused and don't understand, I will remember that You are good and in control. Amen.

DAY 334

Mary and the Empty Tomb

John 20:10-14

The men had gone home. Now Mary Magdalene stood alone at the cave. She was crying. She missed Jesus more than anything. Mary peeked into the cave one last time to see where Jesus had been. The cave was no longer empty. There were two angels inside sitting where Jesus had been. And the angels wanted to know why Mary was crying. "Someone took Jesus, and I don't know where he is," said Mary. When she turned to look the other way, there he stood . . . Jesus himself. But Mary didn't recognize him.

Dear God, When I feel alone and sad,
You always come to be with me. Amen.

DAY 335

Jesus and Mary

John 20:15-18

Mary Magdalene had be crying a long time, and her eyes were sore. So when she saw a man at the cave, she thought he was the gardener. "Sir," said Mary. "Please tell me where you put Jesus." "Mary," came the voice. This was no gardener—it was Jesus. Mary's heart felt full of love. She went to tell the others what she had seen whether they believed her or not. She would tell them all what Jesus had told her . . . that soon he was going back to Heaven to be with God.

Dear God, Just like Mary, make my heart full of love for You to tell others what I know about You. Amen.

Jesus Appears

John 20:19-23

The disciples were waiting for a friend, a friend who had died. They were waiting for Jesus. The women had told them that Jesus was alive and well. All of a sudden, Jesus appeared and was standing among them. He said, "Peace be with you," and showed them the wounds on his hands and feet. The disciples were filled with joy to see Jesus again.

Dear God, Thank You that You promised to be with us always. That makes me so happy. Amen.

DAY 337

Thomas Believes

John 20:24-29

Thomas was not with the other disciples the first time they saw Jesus alive again. Their story sounded crazy! "Unless I touch the scars on Jesus' hands with my own fingers," said Thomas, "I won't believe he is alive." The very next week, Jesus came. "Thomas," said Jesus, "reach out to touch my hands." Thomas cried out, "My Lord and my God!" Then Jesus said to Thomas, "Now you believe because you see me. But blessed is the one who believes without seeing."

Dear God, When I doubt, thank You
for helping me to believe. Amen.

DAY 338

The Full Net

John 21:1-7

"Any luck?" yelled a man from the shore. The friends had been fishing all night but caught nothing. The man said to throw the net on the other side of the boat. Sure enough—the net was now filled with fish! Now they knew who this man was. It was Jesus on shore. When Peter realized this, he leaped into the water with a splash. Peter starting swimming to shore as fast as he could.

Dear God, Thank You that You never stop showing me more of who You are. Amen.

The Meal of Fish

John 21:8-19

The friends dragged the net onto the beach where Jesus stood. Jesus had made a fire to cook the fish, and what a feast it was! One hundred and fifty-three fish and the net didn't even break. When they finished eating, Jesus turned to Peter. "Do you love me?" said Jesus. "You know I do," cried Peter. "If you do," said Jesus, "then care for my people." Peter knew that Jesus forgave him for not being a good friend when Jesus was taken away. Now Peter had a big job to care for the followers of Jesus.

Dear God, Like Peter I want to care for those You love. Show me how to love others. Amen.

DAY 340

Into Heaven

Acts 1:6-11

Jesus came to visit his friends one last time. He wanted them to be his witnesses. So He told them to tell the good news of God in every corner of the world. Then he was lifted up in a cloud, and they could no longer see him. Two angels were standing on the mountain with the people who were looking into the sky. The angels said, "Just like Jesus went up, he will come back again."

Dear God, Thank You that just as You went up to
Heaven in the clouds, so You'll come again. Amen.

DAY 341

Gift of the Spirit

Acts 2:1-17

Jesus had visited his friends to encourage them and tell them what to do next. It was now their job to tell others about God. So the men and women went into a room. There they prayed for God to make them strong. Suddenly, they heard a loud wind blow through the house. The Spirit of God had come to fill them up. Over each of their heads a little flame appeared. They began to talk in other languages, so God's people from other nations could understand them in their own languages. This was a sign that God the Holy Spirit was with them.

Dear God, You have given us your Spirit to tell our
hearts what to do and to give us strength. Amen.

Peter Heals the Crippled Man

Acts 3:1-8

One day, Peter was going into the temple when he heard a voice. A crippled man was asking for money. Peter said, "I don't have any money." The man looked sad. "But what I do have," said Peter, "I will give you. In Jesus' name, get up and walk." The man stared at Peter not sure what to do. So Peter grabbed his hand. He lifted the man up. Something had changed. The man could now feel his feet. He could stand. More than that, he could leap. The man went leaping into the temple, saying thank you to God.

Dear God, I want to do great things for You. Help me to always be ready to help others. Amen.

Philip Steps Out

Acts 4:32-37; 5:12-16; 8:4-8

The apostles shared all they had with one another. They taught in the street and at the temple. In the name of Jesus, they healed the sick. And more and more people believed. Philip did not forget what Jesus had said about people who were mean. Just brush it off. Time to go somewhere else. So Philip went away to Samaria. He would take the good news of Jesus to the people there.

Dear God, Sometimes You want us to stay and sometimes to move away. I will be ready to do either one. Amen.

DAY 344

The Angel in Jail

Acts 5:12-42

The priests and teachers watched Peter and his friends with long frowns. Were they still talking about Jesus after being told not to? "Throw them in jail," said the priests and teachers. But an angel came at night and opened the jail doors. He told them to keep teaching about Jesus. The next morning the priests and teachers came to find the missing prisoners. They found them still teaching about Jesus and healing sick people. Peter was no longer afraid. "We must obey God over people," said Peter. He and the apostles kept talking about Jesus to anyone who would listen.

Dear God, Nothing can stop Your Gospel story from reaching Your people. Help me be brave to tell it. Amen.

DAY 345

Stephen Stands Strong

Acts 6-7

The church needed some special men to be helpers, and Stephen was chosen. He was wise and full of the Holy Spirit. He was so good at preaching about Jesus that the Jewish leaders got angry. They did not want to hear any more of this Jesus, so they decided to get rid of Stephen. But no matter what mean things they did to him, Stephen stayed close to God and forgave them all.

Dear God, Even when others treat me mean for believing in You, help me to be strong and forgiving. Amen.

DAY 346

Simon the Sorcerer

Acts 8:9-24

Simon the Sorcerer could do all kinds of magic. He boasted to be someone great, too. "Look what I can do," said Simon. The people oohed and ahhed. They thought Simon must have power from God . . . until Apostle Philip came to town. Philip could swap sickness for joy just by saying the name of Jesus. The town of Samaria now knew what real power was. Even Simon the Sorcerer believed in Jesus.

Dear God, The name of Jesus is so powerful that just by saying it makes evil go away. Amen.

The African Ruler

Acts 8:26-40

Philip saw a man in a fancy buggy. It was a rich man from Africa, and he was reading the Bible. Philip asked him, "Does it make sense to you?" The man wanted Philip to help him understand it. So Philip got into the chariot. As they bumped along, Philip told about how Jesus came to save them. While traveling, they came across a place with water. Then and there, he was baptized, and he went on his way happier than ever.

Dear God, Please give me a chance to tell someone else about You very soon. Amen.

DAY 348

Saul

Acts 9:1-6

The disciples who loved Jesus had a problem. A religious man named Saul was on his way to put them in jail. But God came to the rescue. Saul was rushing down the road when a bright light shone around him. Saul fell down to the ground. He was very afraid. Then a voice from Heaven spoke. "Why do you fight me?" said Jesus. "Get up, and go to the city." There was something God wanted him to do. Saul obeyed. His servants had to lead him by the hand because Saul was now blind and couldn't see where he was going!

Dear God, You even came to save Saul who was
fighting You. Thank You for showing mercy. Amen.

DAY 349

An Apostle's Courage

Acts 9:10-16

"I am here, Lord," said Ananias when he heard God call. God wanted the apostle to go help a man down the street, a man whose name was Saul. "But God—" cried Ananias, "Saul is a bad man who wants me in jail!" Yet God told Ananias not to worry; He had a plan. Saul was going to help share the good news of Jesus. Ananias obeyed God even though he was afraid. He stood up and went to find Saul.

Dear God, Give me courage to obey when
I am afraid. I will trust in You. Amen.

DAY 350

Saul the Saved

Acts 9:17-20

Saul was praying. He had been in the city now for three whole days. And still, Saul waited. Still, Saul could not see a thing. There in the darkness, Saul felt two hands touch him. Was this the man God told him to wait for? All of a sudden, Saul could see again . . . and there stood Ananias in front of him. Saul wanted to be baptized right away. Then Saul went to tell as many as he could about Jesus, the Son of God.

Dear God, Thank You for opening our eyes
to know that Jesus is our Savior. Amen.

Tabitha, Dearly Loved

Acts 9:36-41

The men told Peter to come quickly. Something was very wrong. Crying filled the house. "See this lovely coat?" said the women. "Look at this fine robe!" They were all clothes that their darling Tabitha had made when she was still alive. Peter sent everyone out of the room where Tabitha lay. Then Peter prayed. "Arise," said Peter. Her eyes opened, and Tabitha took Peter's hand.

Dear God, You can even make people alive again. You are an amazing God. Amen.

God Welcomes All

Acts 10:9-35

Peter had a strange vision. God said to eat up and not to worry what the food was, where it came from, or what it looked like. All of the food was good, said God. Peter went out to find his friends. He told them he had a vision from God. And Peter knew just what it meant. "God wants us to know," said Peter, "that we must share Jesus with all who want to hear no matter where they come from and no matter what they look like. All are invited into the Kingdom of God."

Dear God, Thank You for inviting all kinds of people all over the world to know You. Amen.

DAY 353

The Earthquake

Acts 16:23-26

Saul got a new name: Apostle Paul. He taught about Jesus in as many countries as he could. He healed, and he baptized. And when Paul was put in jail, he stayed brave. He took the time to write letters to the churches that he had built. It was midnight in the jail when the prisoners heard singing. Paul and Silas were singing and praying to God. Suddenly the jail started to shake. The cell doors flew open. And the chains of all the prisoners fell to the floor.

Dear God, I want to have great adventures with You like Paul did when he told others about You. Amen.

The Prison Guard

Acts 16:26-34

The jail doors had flown open by just a prayer. The guard now trembled with fear. He bowed down in front of the two apostles. "Sirs!" said the guard. "What must I do to be saved?" Paul and Silas said that he just needed to believe in Jesus. They had wounds on their bodies, so the guard washed them and took them to his house for a meal. Then the guard and his whole family were baptized. The jailer was filled with joy because he and his whole family now believed in God.

Dear God, You even turn bad times into good times because You are a wonderful God. Amen.

The Sail to Rome

Acts 27

Paul was in chains once again. He would not stop talking about Jesus. So now they were taking Paul to Caesar, the highest ruler. The boat rocked and swayed. Paul had tried to warn his guards not to sail on, but no one listened. The storm got worse and worse. The crew had given up hope when Paul stood up and said, "Don't be afraid. No one will die." Now every ear listened. Paul told them that an angel had visited him at night and told him so. "We will soon be on an island," said Paul. The crew looked out at the most wonderful sight . . . land ahead!

Dear God, Help me always to have hope and believe what You have said in the Bible is true. Amen.

DAY 356

The Shipwreck

Acts 28

Everyone swam to shore. The island natives were friendly and made them food. Paul got warm by the fire. Just then, a deadly snake came up and bit him! The natives could not believe Paul did not fall over dead. *Surely, this man has the power of God*, they thought. When Paul healed a sick man, the rest of the sick on the island came and were healed, too. When the ship was fixed, they said goodbye and set sail.

Dear God, Wherever I go, I want
to tell others about You. Amen.

DAY 357

Paul Writes the Church

1 Corinthians 1:11-18

Paul wrote to one of the churches he had started: "I have heard that some of you are fighting. You each say you follow different teachers. Let me ask you, friends. Did anyone else but Jesus die for your sins? Weren't you baptized in the name of Jesus? You should follow Him only. I came to you not with nice sounding words but with the plain truth so that you would follow God and not people."

Dear God, When I want to fight with my family or friends, help me remember You died for my sins. Amen.

DAY 358

What Comes First?

1 Corinthians 13:1-3

If I could speak any language in the world and even speak with angels, but I don't love those I speak with, my words are only noise. If I knew everything and was the wisest person in the world or could move mountains just by believing, it would mean nothing if I did not love others, too.

Dear God, If I don't have love, then nothing I do will matter at all. Help me to have love first. Amen.

What Is Love?

1 Corinthians 13:4-8

Love is patient. Love is kind. It does not want what others have. It does not brag. Love is never mean. Love is never selfish. Love does not stay mad. Love forgives. Love is happy with truth and never glad with lies. Love protects. It trusts. And love will always hope. Love never ever, ever gives up. And above all else, love will never fail.

Dear God, It is easy to say I love someone, but help me to show that I really do love them. Amen.

What Is Peace?

Philippians 4:8-9

Think on things that are true. Think on what is fair. Think on what is pure and what is lovely. Whatever is very good—think about these things. And make sure you practice all that you have learned from God. And He will be with you and give you peace.

Dear God, Help my mind to think about
what is pure and fair and lovely. Amen.

DAY 361

James Warns of Anger

James 1:17-20

Every good gift is from God in Heaven. And He chose to give us life through Jesus. So don't get mad easily, but first listen, and then choose your words with care. In this way you act like a child of God.

Dear God, Help me to think about my
words and not to get mad quickly. Amen.

DAY 362

What Is Right?

1 Peter 2:21-24

Jesus did not sin. He said no lies or mean words. When he was hated, he did not hate the person back. When Jesus was hurt, he hurt no other. He left things up to God so that God could judge who was right and who was wrong. Jesus came to heal and to show how to live right.

Dear God, Thank You for sending your Son Jesus to show us how to live. Amen.

Who Is the Light?

1 John 1:5-9; 2:8

God is like the brightest light. The light makes you see and feel safe. When you believe in God, he surrounds you with his light. Then you will become a light too - a light that shines with goodness and love just like Jesus did.

Dear God, You are a light in the darkness of the world. Help me be a light too. Amen.

DAY 364

The First and Last

Revelation 22:12-14

"I am the beginning and the end," says God. "I was the first, and I will be the last." Each will be rewarded for the good things they have done. And if you believe in Jesus with all of your heart, you will enter into Heaven and have eternal life.

Dear God, You are the first and the last of all things.
Help me to believe in You and obey your words. Amen.

DAY 365

The Joy of Heaven

Revelation 21:4-22:5

When we get to Heaven, there will be no more dying and no more sadness. God will wipe away all our tears. The great city in Heaven is made of pure gold, and the gates are made of pearls. God will be the light, and we will live there forever with Him.

Dear God, Heaven is so wonderful, and it will be so great to be there with You. Amen.

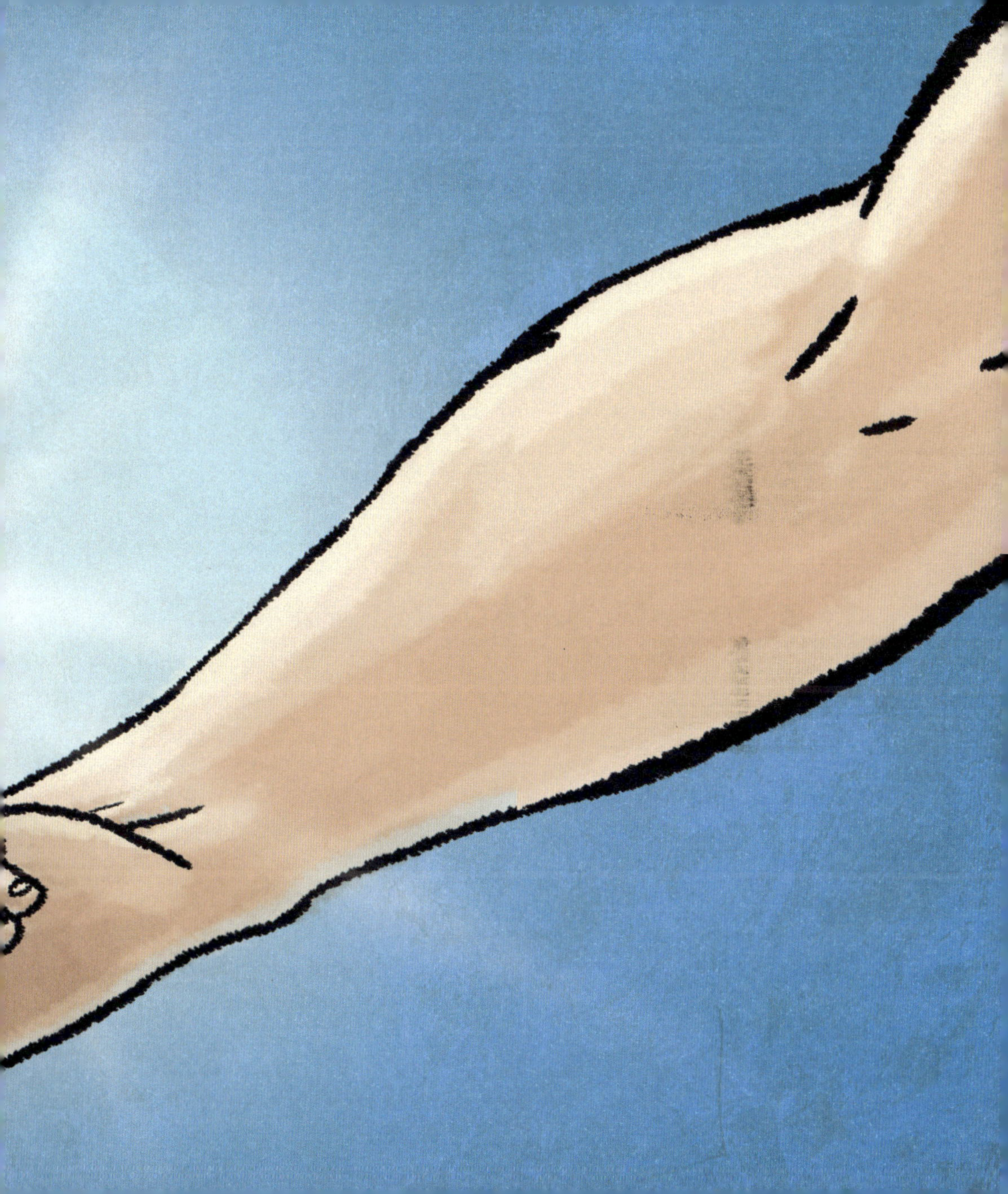